Travel isn't always pretty. It isn't always comfortable. Sometimes it hurts, it even breaks your heart. But that's okay. The journey changes you; it should change you. You take something with you. Hopefully you leave something good behind.

—*Anthony Bourdain*
1956–2018

"There is a curiosity, an eagerness to pursue—and embrace—the unfamiliar, that runs through the stories in this lively collection, much like the spirit of the San Francisco Bay Area itself. No matter where each story takes you, the great joy of this book is knowing that unexpected moments and transformations will be your traveling companions."

—Andy Murdock, co-founder of The Statesider and former U.S. Digital Editor, Lonely Planet

"They may not have realized it when they embarked upon this project, but the members of BATW have brought us the world at a time when so many of us have been forced to stay home. These stories take us to places we might not reach ourselves, show us our shared humanity and evoke the unpredictable wonder of travel. These illuminating tales will tide us over until it's safe to roam again and remind us why we love to travel in the first place."

—Michael Shapiro, author of The Creative Spark and A Sense of Place

"The time to travel is now—in our armchairs, at least—with this heartfelt new collection of travel essays. Learn about wine grapes being grown in Detroit, share a remembrance of sickness in Italy, reimagine a life on the edge in a trip to a remote Canadian wilderness. Full of wit and charm, these mini-memoirs make us yearn to travel again, to find a deeper meaning in all our adventures to come."

—Novella Carpenter, author of Farm City: The Education of an Urban Farmer

"Like travel itself, these essays made me gasp, laugh—and yes, cry. Evocative and beautifully crafted, they transcend genre to limn our known world in surprising new ways."

—James M. Tabor, New York Times bestselling author of Blind Descent and The Deep Zone

TRAVEL STORIES

of WONDER and CHANGE

From Members of Bay Area Travel Writers

Travel Stories of Wonder and Change
Copyright © 2021 Bay Area Travel Writers

Bay Area Travel Writers
www.BayAreaTravel Writers

Photographs:
© LisaAlpine 24; ©Barbara Barrielle 29, 35; ©Robert W. Bone 38, 4i; ©Rosie Cohan 44; ©Monica Conrady 52, 55; ©Diane Covington-Carter 58; ©Lee Daley 64; ©Laura Deutsch 4; ©Ginger Dingus 70; ©Bill Fink 82; ©Judith Horstman pg. vi; ©Laurie McAndish King 76, 88; ©David Laws pg. x, 94,152; ©Diane LeBow 102; ©Effin Older pg. xvi, 110; ©Jules Older 3; ©April Orcutt 10; ©Donna Peck 116; ©Alec Scott 122; ©Jim Shubin front cover, xvii; ©Anne Sigmon 17; ©Carole Terwilliger Meyers 134; ©John Williamson pg. v.

Cover and book design: Jim Shubin
Edited by: Bob Cooper, Jim Gebbie, Judith Horstman, David Bruckmann,
       Amy Sherman and Alec Scott

ISBN: 978-1-7348251-5-2

Dedication

To Lee Foster, our longtime colleague, mentor and cheerleader, whose generosity and kindness made him a beloved friend of many. Lee's skills as a photographer and journalist set him apart. In a life well lived, he taught us so much.

Near Cabo da Roca, Portugal,
westernmost point in continental Europe

Oh, the Places You'll Go!

There is an unintended wistfulness about the travel stories in this collection. They were submitted just as the coronavirus pandemic surged, bringing global travel to a standstill.

We could not have imagined when we conceived this book in January 2020 that a virus would change so much, and so quickly; that soon, millions would be grounded, borders closed, events canceled and whole cities held hostage as global economies faltered.

But our members' memories of travel adventures endure. This book celebrates them, captured in stories from five continents and more than a few islands, on land and at sea. And "stories" they properly are, about journeys to wild places in Canada, China and California; boat trips in the South Pacific, the South Atlantic and the upper Amazon River; and a visit to vineyards springing up in the unlikely vacant lots of downtown Detroit.

Tellingly, as we were locked in isolation, the majority of travel stories submitted featured encounters with the people we met around the globe. Among them: a walk with a child down a dusty road in Madagascar, a bus ride with locals in the Philippines, a negotiation for jewelry in Tibet and the purchase (reluctantly) of a rug in Turkey. Writers recalled a New

Year's Eve party in Egypt, a rescue in a Moroccan bazaar and the kindness of strangers in Ireland, Italy and more.

In a time when travel was frozen, these stories remind us that the greatest gift of travel is not the scenery, spectacular though that may be. It's the understanding and appreciation of "other" that it fosters. "Travel is fatal to prejudice, bigotry and narrow-mindedness, and many of our people need it sorely on these accounts," wrote the well-traveled Mark Twain. May we have it again—soon.

This book would not have been possible without the generous contributions of so many people. An extensive Acknowledgments section properly credits and details their contributions and our gratitude to all, especially the panel of 12 distinguished judges who evaluated the dozens of submissions. The selection process is also described there.

Special thanks are due to BATW's own Georgia Hesse, who didn't let a broken hip deter her from choosing one winner and two honorable mentions for the newly created Georgia Hesse Prize. The Georgia Hesse Prize goes to Laura Deutsch for "Rhythms of Arezzo," with Honorable Mentions for April Orcutt's "Tibetan Bargain with a Twist" and Anne Sigmon's "Sierra Point."

Georgia demonstrates excellence in travel writing for us in a section we call "Master Class," where she writes about the North Pole, the rainforests of Borneo and the seamy port city of Macau. Her fellow renowned travel journalist, Don George, gives us an appreciation of Georgia and her work.

Catharine Hamm, longtime travel writer and editor, most recently for the *Los Angeles Times*, contributes a thoughtful prologue about our next steps as travel journalists. She also helped choose the finalists for the Georgia Hesse Prize.

As we sent this book to press, the global pandemic situation was still grim. It may take a long time—if ever—before travel becomes once again an open and easy way to explore our planet. We suspect it will be very different from what we have known so far this century. We suspect it may humble us and make us grateful for the privileges we have had.

But we professionals are optimistic about the future of travel, whatever it will be. We have to be, as we are driven to explore. As Jules Older writes in his essay, "Goers and Stayers," those two tribes are as different as day and night. We are the "goers."

To finish the Dr. Seuss quote in the headline:

"Oh, the places we'll go! There is fun to be done! ...And when things start to happen, don't worry, don't stew. Just go right along, you'll start happening too!"

—*Judith Horstman*
President, Bay Area Travel Writers

Mormon Barn, Jackson Hole, Wyoming

Where Do We Go from Here?

In travel writing circles, we often debate what our job is after a disaster has devastated a much-loved destination.

"It is to promote the place to help it bounce back!" one side says. The other responds, "No! It is to report on what it's like now, what is gone and what has come back!"

I have thought often about this discussion since the coronavirus descended and threatened to undo the underpinnings of our profession. Our world has been reduced, in many cases, to our homes and our home offices. How do we write about the joy of discovery when the unknown is frightening and human contact can be fatal? What is our job now? Indeed, do we even have a job?

We do, but that job, like the world, has changed. The substance of what we do next may not be clear, but the fact of it is not in question.

The world still needs you to affirm that its wonders await. We need you to be present for the rosy fingers of dawn and dusk, not so you can write about every sunrise and sunset but to help a visitor understand how light paints different pictures at different times of day that make a complete portrait.

Travelers still need your expertise to provide the keys that unlock a destination's mysteries beyond standard suggestions and provide a connection with the soul of the place.

And readers? They need your prose to dance upon the page so that even if they never dance upon that ground, they will have felt the joy of rhythm.

Each of you is positioned to do this. I know this because I have seen your work and it has reminded me of the one thing I learned when I paid attention to business classes: The first rule of creating a successful enterprise is to do what you do well.

Same goes for human beings. And judging by the work you have shared, you already know what you do well because you are doing it.

But that was B.C.—Before COVID-19. How can that still be true?

Because you bring to this equation something we rarely acknowledge but that suffuses our work, whether it is a piece on finding the best travel bargains, the thrill of hearing opera on a gentle night at Sydney Harbour or the surprising majesty of green winter wheat as it waves in a Kansas field.

Pre-pandemic or post-, your prose gives us something that few other genres can: a sense of hope, not for the over-hyped sight that can never match our imaginations but for the possibilities that lie just around that as-yet unturned corner. That is the core of the world's fascination with travel. You bring that to the page, and you make it real.

That is your power. That is your magic. That is your job. Now go and do what you do well.

—*Catharine Hamm*

Catharine Hamm recently retired from the *Los Angeles Times,* where she served 17 years as travel editor. Hamm has three times received individual Lowell Thomas Awards, and the *Times'* travel section was recognized nine times during her tenure as editor. She is President of the SATW Foundation and is a past president of the SATW (Society of American Travel Writers).

CONTENTS

STORIES

MASTER CLASS

Palace Hotel, San Francisco

Goa Gajah Temple, Bali

We have chosen to open the offerings in this anthology with an essay by award-winning writer Jules Older for reasons that will, we hope, shortly become obvious. In it, he divides us mortals into tribes of goers and stayers, speaking of the common traits that unite his tribe, the goers. He asks: What compels some of us to push outward into the world, to go far, to feed a hunger for knowledge about how things are done elsewhere?

Goers and Stayers

Jules Older

As more and more folks seek their tribes, let me add one more tribe to the list. It's more significant than Jewish or Buddhist, Italian or Iranian, male or female, maybe even gay or straight.

I'm talking goers and stayers.

I come from a town of stayers—Baltimore, Maryland— or as the stayers call it, Ballamer Murrilun. Nearly everybody I grew up with in what was then rigidly segregated (by religion and money as well as race), Ballamer was white and Jewish. We went to the same few elementary schools, junior highs, high schools. We dressed pretty much the same, used the same slang, dated the same girls. Even Orthodox families occasionally ate what the rest of us ate—Murrilun crabs, Harley's sandwiches, fresh corn on the cob. We all drank National Bohemian beer.

And, with few exceptions—yes, I'm one of 'em—they all stayed. My friends married girls who lived within a two-mile radius of where they grew up, and still today, they live in that same, safe circle.

So, I come from a place of stayers. Now, I live in a city of goers—San Francisco. My friends here are other goers; they're from China, India, Jamaica, Mexico and Spain; from Massachusetts, Minnesota and Pennsylvania. They're straight and gay, religious (Baptist, Buddhist, Greek Orthodox, Jain, Jewish, Lutheran) and questioning (atheist, agnostic, "spiritual" and "truly, don't care"), with skin the colors of the human rainbow.

In background, we're wildly divergent, but we share one commonality—every one of us, of our own volition, came here from somewhere else. In my case (really, *our* case, since my Vermont farmer's-daughter wife is another goer), we've gone to other places as well; New York City, the South Island of New Zealand, a northern Vermont village of 50.

So, if goers are significantly different from stayers, what makes us different? A lot. Here's my partial list:

We're obviously bolder, but we're also more ruthless. We goers walked out on home and family despite our mothers' tears, our sisters' entreaties, our fathers' stern disapproving glares. We left Anatevka. As well as Bombay and Montego Bay, Nanjing and Deerfield.

We are far, far more curious. As our Deerfield-born friend told us after a visit home, "They still eat at the same restaurants, still play golf at the same club and they never—not once—asked me about my life in San Francisco."

Here in San Francisco, we goers dine Persian, Taiwanese, Mexican, Szechuan, Italian and American. And want to know as much as we can about art in Beijing and the last Indian election.

We goers are also braver. We've been the only non-French speaker at Quebec parties; the only Asian at bar mitzvahs, bat mitzvahs, even faux mitzvahs; the only Pakeha eating muttonbird, the only CFA (come-from-away) chowing down on seal flipper.

And, by definition, we travel more. There's not one of us without a current passport. A fair number have two. A few have three. We use them. Yes, to visit family in Nanjing, but also to explore the Greek islands, kayak with humpback whales in Newfoundland, go on photo expeditions to Mongolia and help bring potable water to the Samburu in Kenya.

We also partner up with folks who most definitely are not the boy or girl next door. Indian and Spanish. Mexican and San Franciscan. Jamaican and Nigerian. Californian and Kenyan. Chinese and German. In our case, the now tame (but then, wildly bold) combo of Ballamer Jewish and Vermont Congregationalist.

Stayers and goers; we're as different as day and night or, as we say in New Zealand, chalk and cheese. We're a tribe, all right, a tribe I'm proud to belong to.

My tribe, New Zealand

On the streets of Arezzo. piazza

The Rhythms of Arezzo

Laura Deutsch

Ten ancient Italians with snow-white hair are lined up on gurneys in the corridor of San Giuseppe Hospital. Ten ancient Italians and me.

Hovering over the adjacent gurney, a man in his mid-forties strokes his mother's hair, "*Mamma, mamma. Madonna mia!*" Sobbing and soothing.

This was not part of my plan. I had jetted across the Atlantic to lead a weeklong writing workshop in Tuscany. After that I would grab an express train and travel the length of Italy's boot, from Puglia on the heel to Como on the cuff, to write a series of articles.

But when I arrived in Arezzo, I found myself soaking in fever-twisted sheets, staring at the hotel room ceiling. Fortunately, this being Italy, the ceiling was frescoed with flowers and birds.

Every morning, Franca, the hotel owner, would knock on my door. Shaking with effort, I would stand, put a shirt over my nightgown and open the door.

"*Buongiorno,* Laura! *Come stai?*" she'd burst like a firecracker.

"*Molto malata,*" I'd gasp. Very sick.

"*Ma meglio, no?*" But better, right? Like she was at a pep rally.

I'd stayed with Franca the year before, racing from hill town to hill town, no time for a wave or a "*ciao.*" Gianni and Marco, owners of antique stores on the piazza, would call out as I flew past. "Laura, *come va?*" How are you?

"*In ritardo!*" Late! I'd shoot back, dashing to catch a bus or train.

Now Franca stared at a hollow-eyed ghost.

Franca's voice was raspy deep, the ashtray at her desk in the hotel lobby heaped with butts of Marlboros. I could hear her chatting in the street as she crossed the Piazza Grande to our hotel, her voice a slow whir and drone like a machine that's stuck, an Army tank crawling over rough terrain.

She brought me liters of water, boxes of broth, pears and yogurt. And a house call from *il dottore.*

He didn't speak English, forcing my meager Italian in unexpected directions. *Ospedale, sangue, laboratorio.* Hospital, blood, laboratory. I told him I thought it was my *rene,* pointing to my kidney.

"Does this hurt?" I presume he asked with a fierce karate chop to my right kidney. It did. I asked that he order lab tests, but "*molto difficile,*" he said. If I needed that, I should go to the hospital.

Two days later, Franca took me to the emergency room where I lay on a white metal bed awaiting my turn. After tests, the doctor mimed her concern, holding up photos of my inner organs, her mouth turned down in exaggerated sadness. I imagined hand-painted Pagliacci tears as she released me six hours later with a sheaf of prescriptions and admonitions, in operatic and incomprehensible Italian, about my kidney infection and possible surgery if antibiotics didn't resolve the problem.

The next morning, my workshop began. Five minutes in, my head dropped to the desk.

"Shouldn't you be in bed?" one of my students asked. I handed her my lesson plans and writing exercises.

Barely able to climb the stone stairs to my room, I felt my Type-A will had been surgically removed. I'd invested so much in this venture, and now I'd have to cancel.

At the end of the first day, the students knocked on my door. "We're having a wonderful time and going ahead with the workshop as planned. Your lessons, your excursions."

They were moving forward, and so would I.

"Tomorrow, do this exercise," I exhaled like Darth Vader, drawing a mind map on a sheet of butcher paper to illustrate. "See the Piero della Francesca frescoes, then write using this prompt."

So began our routine. *I will do my job*, I insisted to myself, pulling every ounce of energy into instructing students how to lead each other in the daily lessons. I wrote out exercises and drew maps of the towns they would visit without me.

I focused on each in-breath to punch out short phrases. "In Orvieto. Follow this lane. Twelfth-century church. Faded frescoes." I handed out a guided meditation. "Read this and sit for 10 minutes. Then write, starting with this line."

They'd telephone to tell of their breakthroughs. I'd issue edicts from my bed then mentally draft my obituary. After classes, they'd wake me from coma-like sleep: "Still having a wonderful time."

Each evening at 7:p.m. the men of our neighborhood gathered at the corner of the piazza, beneath my hotel window. Echoing on the cobblestones, I could hear the basso profundo of *il dottore*, checking in with his friend Gianni.

I listened to their voices, and I listened to the bells, the rhythms, of Arezzo. The first night I thought, *Surely the bells will stop at midnight.* The second night I thought, *Surely this clanging will drive me insane.* The third, exhausted, I slept through the rings that let all Arezzo know another 15 minutes had elapsed.

I am a take-charge person, but I surrendered to the bells. Unable to sit, stand or eat, I couldn't pack and get to the airport, let alone have a sit-down with the madman who'd programmed the bells. I emailed my doctor in the U.S. and called close friends back home. Lie low and recover, we decided.

Periodically, I dragged myself downstairs in the evening to speak to *il dottore*. With pen and paper, he drew a kidney so I would understand what was happening. With my dictionary between us, we "discussed" my latest lab results. Blocked kidney, infection, more tests required.

The students departed when the workshop ended. Frightened, I hugged my last ride to Rome goodbye. My week in Arezzo grew into a month. Trains left day after day without me, headed for the olive harvest in the south and tranquil lakes in the north.

I wanted to push on, and I wanted to stay. "Laura, remain near the doctors and labs that you know," Franca said, granting the permission I needed to rest.

I graduated from liquids to gruel to solid food once a day. At a takeout place on Corso d'Italia, I found homemade soups, vegetables and salads. My vocabulary blossomed with the bounty of the season: spinach, beets, green beans. At night, I looked up words to fine-tune the next day's requests. *Latte scremata* (skimmed milk). *Pasta fatta in casa* (homemade pasta). I was learning to conjugate verbs. Soon I would have a past and a future, a trace of personality.

When I had the strength to walk across the sloping piazza, I limped uphill to the *biblioteca*, a 15th-century library that had been Wi-Fied for me, and 100 Italian students. Together we marinated in the overheated reading room while early winter storms beat against the leaded windows.

"*Lento, lento*"—slowly, slowly—Gianni called out as I thumped past his door, leaning on the walking stick I'd brought to conquer mountain trails. "*Piano, piano*"—slowly, slowly—Marco waved as I passed his shop. I paused to greet his 80-year-old parents, seated on a bench overlooking the piazza.

"*Buona sera. Come state?*"

I sat with them as neighbors gathered for their evening stroll. Franca offered me a gelato. *Il dottore* ambled down from his office. My emails could wait. For now, I was living in Arezzo.

The author with an extraordinary Tibetan woman, Gele,
and Gele's son in Lhasa, Tibet

Tibetan Bargain with a Twist

April Orcutt

"Please! Please!" the Tibetan woman pleaded, her young son trailing behind her. She approached me in the ancient market of Lhasa, the capital of Tibet, holding an orange beaded necklace that hung around her neck, smiling sweetly as she implored me to buy it.

But I didn't want orange beads. I was on an extended solo trip through Asia and, wanting to travel as long as possible, had to be judicious with my spending.

"No, thank you," I said.

"Please!" she said. It must have been the only word she knew in English.

"No. *Tu-jay-chay.*" It was the only word I knew in Tibetan. "Thank you."

"Please!"

China had opened Tibet for independent travel only three months before, so my Western face was a novelty. Or maybe she sensed that I love unusual jewelry.

"Please!"

She was insistent yet endearing, with her lovely smile and that mischievous twinkle in the eye that is unique to Tibetans. Red and brown yarn twisted through long, black hair piled onto her head, and, in front, a few strands threaded through four small turquoise beads. A rough black sash with pockets hung over her pink-striped blouse and gray skirt, and a small pouch secured with string peeked out above it. Her son, who was about nine, stood silently at her side, a threadbare brown jacket over his red shirt and an unsure look on the face peering below the brim of his gray cap.

Again I said, "No," to beads—but I pointed to the bracelets on her wrist.

She removed one: a strip of twisted brass, twisted again with copper and silver, and shaped into a rustic cuff.

"One yuan," I said, holding up my index finger. It was a ridiculously small sum. About 50 U.S. cents.

"Oh!" She was shocked. Or she feigned shock. I saw that twinkle in her eye. She held up 10 fingers, no, 10 again—20.

"Twenty yuan?!" I stepped back. That was 10 bucks—a fortune in backpacker-travel-money. "Oh, no, no!" I said. "Two yuan," two fingers.

She pretended to be horrified. Then she indicated "18 yuan."

This dance continued, each of us alternately pretending to be offended at the other's offer and tendering a new price. We grinned, laughed and settled on six yuan.

That was fun, and I loved the bracelet. I pointed to another and off came the twisted brass, copper and silver design, smoothed into one solid piece. We repeated our game, faster this time and with fewer dramatics and even more smiles, our eyes meeting with laughter, but we got to the same place, six yuan.

Next I bought a silver ring. Our opening offers were not so far apart this time, and we completed our transaction quickly.

Behind us, Lhasa's denizens, nomads and worshipers from across Tibet ambled around the Old Town of Lhasa— the Barkor, the maze of dirt alleys twisting among 700-year-old stone buildings encircling the most important Buddhist temple in Tibet, the Jokhang. Many Tibetans twirled brass prayer wheels, small cylinders revolving on shafts, each spin offering a prayer for compassion. For more than 13 centuries Tibetan pilgrims have reverently circled the Jokhang Temple, always clockwise, always with the temple off their right shoulder, each half-mile circuit a prayer.

I gestured toward the procession, and my new Tibetan friend, her son and I joined the throng. We strolled through the alleys, smiling, laughing and surveying bells, prayer flags, saddle blankets for yaks and hand-loomed fabric in stripes of fuchsia, ocher, indigo and emerald.

Pilgrims stretched out full body-length on the dirt road, marked where their extended hands touched, stood up, moved their feet to where their hands were and repeated the process as they circled the temple and the Barkor. Some used the same grueling technique to circumambulate Mount Kailas, the holiest mountain in Tibet—a distance of 33 miles. We looked at each other and nodded with respect toward the pilgrims.

Her son's eyes, wide open, followed a man who whirled a paper cone around the inside edge of a circular metal pan, accumulating white spun sugar with each twist. I bought cotton candy for the three of us, and the boy beamed.

I photographed my friend with her arm around her son, and I asked someone else to take a photo of the three of us in the square in front of the Jokhang.

My friend led us toward the Jokhang, past a dozen Tibetans prostrating themselves at its entrance, and into its candle-lit darkness with the pungent odor of burning yak butter, the rancid aroma that permeates Tibetan temples, blended with juniper incense. For two hours, we silently turned dozens of prayer wheels, again and again. We were the energy source spinning golden cylinders engraved with prayers and sending those prayers to the heavens. So many wheels, so many prayers....

Rejoining the circuit, we stopped at a Tibetan merchant's table. The merchant spoke English. He had left Tibet as a child many years before, and now that China had opened the border with Nepal, he returned as a businessman.

"Your friend's name is Gele," he said. "She has a 16-year-old daughter, who is on a pilgrimage to Mount Kailas. Gele is a recent widow, and she's trying to move from Chamdo in eastern Tibet to Kathmandu in Nepal." She had traversed half of her 1,000-mile journey. I said I was impressed.

Gele reached into her pouch and brought out a one-inch, camel-shaped brass pendant. Its plain surface was worn smooth, and a hand-braided string looped through a hole in its center. "She said this was made by the gods and dropped from the sky," the shopkeeper said. "I can tell it is very old."

The magical story intrigued me—I bought the amulet for a few yuan, a price I thought was too low, but she wouldn't go higher.

"She says you've helped her a great deal on this journey because you've bought so much of her jewelry, and now she has money to travel." I asked him to tell her how much I treasured her jewelry.

He said she wanted to meet the next day so I asked where and at what time. He said not to worry. "She will find you. These people are very clever."

She did find me. Again we circumambulated the Barkor three or four times.

I pointed to her squared-off brass ring with a small turquoise stone in the center. She took it off. It was rustic with rough edges, sturdy with geometric patterns engraved around the stone. And I wanted to help her with her trek—although the distances were shorter, her travels were more monumental than mine. If I had to cut my trip short by a few days, I would survive. It was she who was beginning a new life, or who would be if she could get herself and her son to Nepal. I would offer her earlier starting price.

I held up 10, then 10-again fingers. "Twenty yuan," I said. She shook her head. No, no, no. She held up one finger. "What?" I asked. I held up one finger. "One yuan?" She nodded.

"Oh, no, no," I said, shaking my head. "Twenty! Twenty yuan!" Ten-plus-10 fingers.

One finger.

Twenty fingers.

I held out 20 one-yuan bills. She took one. I gave her the others. She pushed them away.

"No!" I said. "You must take more!" We laughed. But she wouldn't take more. In bargaining throughout the world I'd never encountered such a thing—she was refusing my higher price. Surely she could use the money. But she had enough for her needs. I was stunned—I could only look at her and smile in amazement.

We walked again, watching the pilgrims, smelling the juniper incense, hearing the prayer wheels spin. Then Gele *gave* me her last bracelet....

The author climbing to Sierra Point

Sierra Point

Anne Sigmon

"So," Jack said. "When are we going to have a real date?" He reached across the table and rested his hand on mine. Our pulses touched with magnetic energy.

"Not long," I said.

That was April 1991, the night Jack and I met over the strains of Wagner at a symphony outing arranged by a Presbyterian singles group. No dewy-eyed novices, we'd both been married before. He was 50; I was 38.

After our first "real" date at the French bistro-of-the-moment, after Mozart at the Opera, after a picnic with my dogs—my choice—Jack suggested a camping trip to Yosemite National Park with a hike to Sierra Point, his favorite spot.

I hesitated. "I haven't hiked much."

That was an understatement. Not counting walking my dogs in the park, I'd never hiked at all.

All my life I'd fantasized about traveling to exotic, physical places—chugging up the Umba River on the *African Queen* or teetering on the edge of a Colombian jungle waterfall. Trouble was, I'd never had the courage or the physicality for it. Painful experience—including the humiliation of flunking junior high P.E. —had taught me to shy away from anything that smacked of physical prowess. Already in my late thirties, I couldn't foresee any miraculous improvement. Now Jack wanted to take me to Yosemite to walk in the footsteps of Ansel Adams. I couldn't say "no." A fair warning would have to do.

"I'm not at *all* athletic," I emphasized, not mentioning that I was also terrified of heights. My omission seemed reasonable. I didn't want to scare him off with graphic descriptions of my klutziness just as our relationship was gaining traction.

"No problem, we'll take it easy," Jack promised. "You'll love it." His blue eyes danced.

On hike day, we set out early, leaving behind wood smoke and coffee smells and the clatter of the Upper Pines campground coming to life. As we crossed the footbridge leading to the John Muir Trail, my white leather tennis shoes crunched on the gravel path and squished in the wet dirt. They also pinched my toes. I snuggled in my parka against the morning chill and the pink-green-blue mist swirling at the base of Vernal Falls.

Excited about Jack, already in love with the mountain, I ignored my anxiety about the physical demands. *Just don't think about it* was my mantra.

My twill pants whooshed as we climbed through dry brush looking for the unmarked path to Sierra Point. I couldn't see anything that looked like a trail—just a mass of boulders surrounded by an impenetrable thicket of manzanita briars. My shirt caught on the briars, my shoes slipped on the rocks. My manicured nails snapped. I pushed myself to keep up but soon fell behind Jack's easy stride.

"I'll go on ahead to check the trail," he said. I nodded, panting to catch my breath. My heart was kabooming from exertion and altitude when I stopped for a sip of water. The sun blinded me as I craned my neck. Jack was 50 feet ahead and above me, up a steep ravine, half-hidden by a ponderosa pine. He slouched lazily against the tree glassing for eagles, giving me a chance to catch up. To reach him, I'd have to inch across the creek bed, squeeze around building-sized boulders and clamber, climb or crawl over a granite rock-fall that hung by the edge of a cliff to nowhere.

Another woman might have stopped right there, might have called him out: *Are you nuts? Weren't you listening? I'm a beginner!* Another woman, maybe a woman with more sense, might have turned back. But I wasn't that woman. I was a striver. Underneath it all, I longed to be the kind of woman who *could* do this. I cussed and fussed under my breath. Was I fuming at Jack for dismissing my limitations? Or at myself for feeling constrained by them?

Through all the grumbling self-doubt, I kept on climbing. Up and up, through towering pine, spruce and fir, past blooming dogwood and—at last finding the trail—up broken steps almost a century old. Following the path of Ansel Adams!

Jack poured on gentle encouragement. "You're doing great. Almost there."

The forest smelled of moss and mist and pungent bay laurel. I scooched over a boulder and followed the trail onto an overhang that seemed barely wider than my shoe. Pine needles camouflaged roots tailor-made to trip me. My palms were damp; my heart was thumping. I held my breath. After one quick glance down at the Merced River snaking a thousand feet below, I murmured a quick prayer and didn't dare look again.

My legs felt weak, my stomach was queasy. Still breathing hard—now from fright—I followed close behind Jack as he pushed through a stand of fir trees onto a narrow ledge. I grabbed a spindly pine branch—for what, security?—as I followed him forward. I stopped cold four feet from oblivion, first in terror, then in amazement.

Beyond the fir trees, the ledge broadened into an overhang like a crow's nest. Suddenly the sun was on my face. The wind whipped my parka around me. Above and below and to my right and left, waterfalls roared and tumbled white and wild into the Merced River: Vernal, Nevada, Illilouette, Upper and Lower Yosemite. Granite monoliths carved by eons of glacial creep soared three thousand feet over my head. That ledge seemed like a perch at the base of heaven.

Jack dropped his daypack by a scraggly pine. He held out a hand, and I inched toward him.

My pounding heart began to slow. My fear of heights, the strain of the climb, my terror at teetering at the edge of the precarious trail were replaced by the pure magnificence of this eagle's-nest view.

"Well, what do you think?"

"Terrifying...magnificent...stupendous!"

He grinned. "Told you you'd love it. This is the only place in Yosemite where you can see four waterfalls."

We sat at the base of the tree, not talking much for a few minutes, letting the place sink in.

This spot, we learned, was steeped in history. For years,

naturalists had searched for a single vantage point to view Yosemite's five great waterfalls. One of the Valley's early rock climbers used triangulation to identify this as the likely place. He made the first known ascent on June 14, 1897, and named it Sierra Point in honor of the Sierra Club. Years later, Ansel Adams climbed up, according to his notebooks, and took some of his early photographs from this spot. Bridalveil is the only one of Yosemite's great falls not visible from Sierra Point.

Jack and I drank in the view, followed by a lunch of brie and baguette. In that pre-digital era, we snapped off almost a roll of film then balanced the camera unsteadily on a rock to take a photo of ourselves.

Afterward, he flipped through his dog-eared, 10-year-old hikers' guide to read me the trail description. The steep climb of one-and-a-half miles was described as "four equivalent miles." I didn't dispute that!

When Jack finished, I picked up the book and read on until I saw this warning: "Due to the steepness of the climb, it is fairly strenuous...if you should find yourself off-trail, retrace your steps at once as there are nearly vertical cliffs below almost all the trails."

As I closed the book, a printer's addendum in the flyleaf caught my eye. "The Sierra Point Trail has now been closed as too dangerous."

I looked at Jack. "Just an easy hike, huh?"

He scrunched his face into a you-caught-me pout. "I'm sorry. It seemed easier the last time I was here." Then: "Are you glad you came?"

I thought for less than a second. "Absolutely."

And I meant it.

In my sheltered experience of parking-lot viewpoints, I'd never seen anything like this, never been anywhere like Yosemite. And I'd never met anyone like Jack.

But one lesson I might've learned that day didn't quite sink in. It was a lesson I learned gradually, after we crashed our canoe in the whitewater of the Pigeon River in Michigan, after we surprised a grizzly bear fishing on the Alagnak River in Alaska, dodged rhesus monkeys cannonballing our boat as we inched through a Borneo jungle and galloped bareback on Mongolian ponies across the steppe.

That lesson: Traveling to the wild with Jack often—no, usually—resembles a boot camp in exotic places. But I keep coming back, back, back again because over the years I've learned: The wonder of wild places with Jack fills my heart; overcoming my own limitations feeds my soul.

The thermals of a timeless sky in Morocco are
crowded with birds

The Dancing Birds of Fez

Lisa Alpine

It is not until I leave the interior of the Fez medina and drive the perimeter road circling the ancient fortress walls that I observe the large, pterodactyl-like bird skimming by the car and over the olive groves marching up the hillside. To my left, a verdant riverbed below it bristles with waterfowl who eye the impressive bird with as much awe as I do.

"*Qu'est-ce que c'est?*" I ask my guide, pointing up at the sky.

He does not notice the bird. He's avoiding slamming into on overburdened donkey that is oblivious to all the cars whizzing past as it shuffles across the four lanes of traffic.

The bird swoops close to us at eye level. It is huge and dirty-white with coal-black wings that spread out two meters. As it gracefully flaps by in slow motion, a hefty catfish wriggles in its gigantic beak.

"A stork!" I yell, flailing my hands. The driver is still not paying attention to me as yet another tipsy, tired donkey steps into the traffic. I recognize the bird as a stork because it looks just like the ones depicted on greeting cards carrying a baby dangling in a cloth diaper from their beaks.

Another stork lifts off from the pollen-heavy cattails crowding the murky stream that runs down the *wadi* (riverbed) next to the road. The sky is filling with storks, and clouds of swallows converge, mingling with the giant, wheeling birds. A hawk hovers—a still point in the dance of the birds—and then, to punctuate the grays of the stork, the tans of the hawk and the silver-blues of swallows' wings glinting in the harsh sunlight, a troupe of pure-white ibis lift off from the reeds and join the circling celebration of birds overhead.

I crane my neck in wonder, amazed that these birds are abundant in Fez in a modern era when pesticides and herbicides have eliminated many species. I feel the timeless being of these birds. Clouds and carpets of birds. The trill and twitter of birdsong alive and well.

"*Alhamdulillah!*" I exclaim. As I utter this eloquent Arabic word that means "praise be to God," my driver looks up at the circling birds and, smiling, says, "*Allah ho Akbar*"— God is great.

I learned a new dance move in Morocco that follows me onto the dance floor whenever I'm possessed by the feeling of freedom, of lifting off to cultures so far from my nest. This gratitude has a shape: My arms rise slowly and stretch into the flying stork with wings outspread, circling with my flock in the thermals of a timeless sky.

One of the many vineyards planted on formerly vacant lots in Detroit's most desolate neighborhoods

Vacant Lot Vineyards

Barbara Barrielle

In the Detroit that has been forgotten, where forlorn neighborhoods were destroyed by economic realities, there are abandoned homes. There are mounds of construction debris, dumped because it's easier than regulated disposal; cars missing wheels and paint and parts; residents with hollow looks and kids playing among the forgotten garbage of vacant lots. And, every now and then, I find a spot of green, a bit of new growth and the manicured trellising reminiscent of a vineyard.

I have worked in the wine industry for more than 20 years. The kind of wine country I'm used to is one of rolling hills and winding roads, with fields of green slowly waving in light winds. Estate homes might dot the landscape and, depending on the time of year, vineyard workers are either pruning the vines coming out of a winter dormancy or, with grape knives flying, picking the ripe grapes and tossing them in bins on the truck following behind their crew.

I have never seen wine grapes growing in a place like Detroit. But here in the blighted, depressed areas of the city, there are now vineyards. Some are butting up against extreme wealth (like the enclave of Grosse Pointe), but most are stuck in a maze of depressed neighborhoods.

These are petite urban vineyards that are new and struggling to take root. At this point, scrawny brown vines with offshoots of green leaves stretch along supporting wire trellises, a couple years from fruiting—but they are undeniably vineyards. In fact, 100,000 vines are planted in Detroit's marginal neighborhoods and, with 80,000 vacant lots in the city, there is plenty more room to grow. There's even a winery downtown, where a Detroit local has grand plans for these seemingly far-fetched plantings.

Well before the time of automobiles—Detroit's most well-known industry over the last hundred years—Frenchman Antoine de la Mothe Cadillac established Detroit's first vineyard. Planted in 1702, it was one of the very first vineyards in North America.

Cadillac found that the grapes he grew here, where Lake Erie, Lake St. Claire and the Detroit River meet, were *"raisins de vigne avec peau mince et tres bon jus qui fera un vin excellent"*—"thin-skinned wine grapes with a juice that will make excellent wine." Because Detroit has those Burgundian-type, fog-influenced growing conditions that come with being close to water—and soil reminiscent of the limestone, clay, gravel and sand necessary for French varietals like Pinot Noir and Chardonnay—it is not unreasonable to make wine here from local fruit.

But before these new petite vineyards, it had been a long time since grapes were planted in Detroit. Called America's Renaissance City, Detroit grew and prospered as it became the home of auto manufacturing for all of the U.S. and much of the world. Thriving from the time it became a city in 1815, Detroit was called "the Paris of the West" for its wealth and culture, beautiful mansions and museums. Shipbuilding then autos fueled growth through most of the 20th century. Detroit's industrial base thrived, but so did much more. Motown, the music that shaped the 1950s and 1960s, was born in

Detroit. When she died two years ago, Aretha Franklin, the "Queen of Soul," came back to "The Motor City" to be buried here.

As happens with economic growth, the population exploded. Civil unrest in the city forced many to move out to the suburbs. The abandonment of downtown Detroit began in the 1980s and continued to increase in the current century. But it was when the recession of 2008 left cars on lots without buyers that the city crumbled in earnest. Once the fourth-largest city in the country, Detroit soon ranked barely 18th.

Many say that Detroit is going through a second "renaissance." Sure, the downtown area is dotted with cranes, soaring hotels and business towers; it's buzzing with new construction. There's a chatter of passersby on the main drag, which is heaving with new restaurants and retail spaces.

But head away from this buzzy scene and it's clear that much of the city is still devastated. In many neighborhoods, those former mansions sit empty, impossible to repair, expensive to fix and slated to be demolished—if they haven't been already. Smaller homes, too, have been abandoned and ripped down, leaving vacant lots. Detroit now has more than 80,000 vacant lots. Many have become dumping grounds. All of them cast a pall on the neighborhoods where residents stuck out the collapse of the city around them, only to be rewarded with crime, loss in property value and little hope for a different future.

But when Blake Kownacki looks at these vacant lots, he sees possibility.

Kownacki was doing fine, making wine and seeing the world as a winemaker: He had a successful career in organic farming then made wine in Paso Robles, California, and Australia. But his roots and family in Michigan were calling him back. So Kownacki, an affable and engaging guy in his forties with a full beard who leads his winery with the directive to "have fun," managed a winery in the Traverse City area—where most Michigan wineries are based—for years. At that point, wineries in Detroit were unheard of. Although historically agricultural, the city of Detroit has not warranted a mention in discussions of winemaking in Michigan.

That was until this year when Detroit Vineyards took the old Stroh's ice cream factory smack in downtown Detroit and made it into a production, event and wine-tasting facility. Though Detroit Vineyards began producing wine in 2016 in Blake's garage, the move to downtown was big: They sit next to the large, historic Eastern Market, so their foot traffic is solid. The winery has been an undeniable success. And as if in a nod to Antoine de la Mothe Cadillac, Detroit Vineyards uses classic French vintner practices of making natural wines that are unfiltered and unrefined.

With a true urban winery, production is onsite. Currently, Kownacki sources fruit from the established American Viticultural Areas (AVAs) in Michigan like Traverse City. But, with the opening of the winery, production will increase from 1,200 to 12,000 cases in a year. While sourcing from established vineyards will surely continue, Kownacki, driven to break the boundaries and defy expectations, has a plan to bring in truly local fruit—grown within the city itself.

Those vacant lots that reflect blight in the city are perfect for small vineyards, says Kownacki. With a price tag of $100 per lot, the land is cheap and the location—as Monsieur Cadillac found 300 years ago—yields excellent grapes. If vineyards are planted on this neglected land and Detroit Vineyards guides neighborhood owners on the planting, care and cultivation of grapevines, it's a win-win for both the winery and Detroit's residents.

"I thought, 'What can our company do to improve this situation' where the revitalization of Detroit has been concentrated on the Woodward Corridor and has left 130 of 140 square miles out of the benefit area," says Kownacki. "We chose to work with the people who remained here and work toward eradicating blight and raising their property values."

As Detroit's urban vineyards continue to grow, Kownacki is getting closer to his dream. But in about 2015, when he first started sitting down with a glass of wine and dropping his "vacant lot vineyard" idea into conversations, nearly everyone dismissed him. It was a ridiculous idea.

Initially, city officials were skeptical. But Kownacki became known as the "one who wouldn't go away." He has moxie and a gut feeling that, little by little, he will break down the resistance of those who dismiss, laugh at or ignore him.

To make Detroit Vineyards a reality, Kownacki partnered with Dr. Claes Fornell, a University of Michigan professor with a small vineyard who served on the Michigan Wine and Grape Council. Kownacki had helped silent partner Dr. Fornell with his small vineyard in Ann Arbor and, over time, their discussions of making wine and growing grapes in the urban center of Detroit became more than fantasy. Dr. Fornell believed in both Kownacki and the project. They would build Detroit Vineyards to be more than just a winery.

"Nine years ago, when I started this project, I was considered crazy," says Kownacki. "Now I am not so crazy... A vacant lot is $100, and we will help you plant and care for a vineyard. Once it is productive, I will buy the fruit—so it is an investment property, beautifies the neighborhood and raises property values. We don't need to own the land; we just want the grapes. That means about $1,500 in the vineyard owner's pocket annually."

It took years to make progress, but with the support of believers like Dr. Fornell, employees who jumped on board and eventually city officials, Kownacki's tenacity began to pay off: The staff at the winery has grown to 20 and, since opening in May 2019, they are barely able to catch their breath between marketing the wine and fielding the media attention.

One of those employees is dedicated to community outreach. I have never seen this position in a winery, especially a small one. That is the commitment of this group.

Shortly after opening, Detroit Vineyards held a community planting party with a DJ, a bouncy house for the kids and BBQ for everyone. They have held urban grape stomps that engage both adults and kids.

"The neighborhood gets into it, digs the project and watches out for the vineyards," Kownacki says. "I am far more worried about birds and deer damaging the vines than I am about people."

Thomas Roberes met Kownacki at the Home Depot where he had a part-time job in 2016, and the two discussed their passion for urban gardening. "We talked, and he wanted to check out my urban garden," Roberes says. "When he saw it, he was amazed and wanted me to work with him on the vineyard project. I was very interested because I have never heard of any idea like this ever being done in this city."

Roberes became Detroit Vineyards' full-time Community Outreach Coordinator in August 2018. The position largely consists of winning people over.

Roberes points to a very skeptical president of the Morningside Community where Detroit Vineyards, with the help of nonprofit U-Snap-Bac, planted the largest urban vineyard to date. After watching Roberes and Kownacki go door-to-door and answer questions, this community leader did an about-face and helped find the space to host their neighborhood planting event.

"After the residents get over the shock factor that a vineyard is being put in their neighborhood, they learn all the benefits of a community vineyard and their shock turns into curiosity," says Roberes. "We base the vacant lot vineyard idea on four goal pillars: eradicate blighted land, increase property value, teach lifelong skill sets and put money back into the resident's pocket."

Detroit Vineyards Outreach Coordinator Thomas Robares plants a vine at one of the vacant lot vineyards.

Detroit Vineyards is focused on shaking up not just the people involved but also the plants. Although in its infancy, its nonprofit planting project is making inroads with 1,000 vines of a cold-tolerant varietal called Marquette, a hybrid cross between a native North American grape and traditional vinifera.

What's more, Kownacki doesn't plan on stopping at vacant lots. He hopes to plant near the water where his analysis shows Burgundian varietals like Pinot Noir and Chardonnay will flourish. He eyes an underutilized waterfront park that would be perfect for grape-growing education and even more community engagement. This, of course, will take even more massaging of city managers. But, Detroit has a history of 150 years of farming and Kownacki loves returning to those roots, making the concept of farming fun and profitable for those interested in participating.

"This is a collaborative community effort. I think I can get 20 tons of fruit from city vineyards," says Kownacki. "I could buy up parcels of land, but that is not how we roll. I want to see individuals who live here, the ones who stayed, benefit from our winery."

At the end of the day, Kownacki's vision is a communal one. The fact that these vineyards are flourishing is due to a collective effort. Kownacki might have been the first to see this kind of hope in Detroit's vacant lots, but he certainly isn't the last.

"Grape growing is not glamorous. It is farming. But I want kids to know that if they have experience in the wine business, they can travel the world. Once you learn the skill set, you can harvest anywhere."

Defensive gun at a cave entrance on Peleliu

The Battle of Peleliu

Robert W. Bone

We fought our way up a difficult jungle rise, grabbing wet tropical foliage that seemed to grab back at us, slapping at bare legs and faces as we slowly moved forward. The day was forebodingly dark. It had been raining on and off, and now it was on again. But Tangie Hesus, our indefatigable Palauan guide, urged our little group onward, promising there was shelter ahead.

Our uphill struggle was nothing compared to the travails of Americans and Japanese more than a half-century earlier. We were exploring the South Pacific island of Peleliu, the scene of one of the bloodiest and perhaps most useless battles of World War II.

The tiny island of Peleliu is today one of the states of Palau. Also spelled Belau, this independent nation of islands in the Caroline group is one of the more recent entries into the United Nations.

Palau is largely unknown to Americans today, except some avid scuba divers. For them, it offers perhaps the cleanest waters and the richest collection of colorful ocean fish in the world.

But the atmosphere at Peleliu, a 20-minute, light-plane ride from Palau's capital of Koror, is different. Here is where thousands died violently or miserably between September 15 and November 25, 1944. Estimates put the toll at nearly 2,000 American soldiers and Marines plus 11,000 of the island's Japanese defenders.

As we grappled our own way up the hill, I thought about stories I had read. Allied commanders, flush with recent victories, thought Peleliu would be a two-day cakewalk and that its airfield would then be a handy base in the coming campaign to retake the Philippines.

They also thought the island was flat. Advance intelligence had failed to discover it was full of rugged hills and ridges into which the Japanese had bored an elaborate system of virtually impenetrable caves and tunnels. At this stage in the war, they were no longer trying to beat back Allied forces on the beaches. Instead, they relied on heavy firepower from camouflaged and well-protected interior positions.

Moreover, President Roosevelt and Prime Minister Churchill had recently met in Quebec and decided that the assault on the Philippines was to begin immediately without further preparation. But the wheels of fate were already in motion. The Peleliu operation was not turned back.

Thunder was now echoing off the hills, sounding a lot like artillery fire. The rain came down harder, and I remembered reading that GIs had come across similar weather conditions a few days into the invasion. With these thoughts in mind, I moved over a muddy rise and suddenly found myself staring into the mouth of one of the greenest, meanest heavy gun barrels I had ever seen, its rifling still apparent after more than 50 years. Except for the moss on its metal surface, it looked ready to fire.

With the accompanying thunder and lightning plus the torrential downpour, the sight was one of the most startling experiences I'd had since we began exploring the island. Sure enough, we found shelter behind the gun, which was mounted at the mouth of one of the thousands of caves still present on the island.

We explored a couple of tunnels and after the rain let up, we made our way past the old cannon and down the hill to return to Tangie's van. Over the next few hours, he took us to other remnants of war—ruins of burned-out blockhouses, wrecks of tanks and planes, the rugged and sharp coral-strewn invasion beaches and various lonely shrines erected by Americans and Japanese in the years following the war.

We also went to a one-room museum where he had gathered an eclectic collection of war's detritus—hand grenades, bayonets, Coke and sake bottles and more, including some poignant reminders of the personal nature of war.

Tangie Hesus and the wreckage of a Japanese Zero

There was an optimistic letter from an American private in Peleliu to his sister, telling her he was in fine health and "not to worry about me" four days before he was killed. And there was a Japanese flag with hand-scrawled characters on it. Tangie translated it for us: "We're just a bunch of boys who know we're going to die, and we miss our mothers."

As we returned to the airfield, Tangie apologized for the bad weather that kept us from some of the more elaborate caves and tunnels. These included one which had housed more than 1,000 Japanese until they were finally killed by a new and more powerful flamethrower that had just entered the war at Peleliu.

We were glad we came, and the rain certainly suited the mood of the place. But we were also happy to leave Peleliu and quickly fly back to Koror and the cheerful and sunny Palau of today.

Like some other places in the world, Peleliu, I thought, should be seen just once—preferably in the rain—and remembered forever.

Goreme, Turkey: A village of caves and fairy chimneys

Ali's Heritage Garden

Rosie Cohan

Pink skid marks faded to purple on the blackening sky as lights popped on across Goreme, the rocky Turkish village below me. I had checked into my room and saw my friend, Ali, sitting alone on the terrace of his hotel which he built within walls of his family's cave home. Cave homes had been a common form of habitation in this rugged land for centuries. Ali's chair was turned toward the valleys on the opposite side of the illuminated village. He was nursing a beer.

"*Iyi aksamlar* (Good Evening). May I join you?" I saw a flash of melancholy disappear from his face as he turned around. We hugged and kissed each other on both checks.

"Why are you sitting here alone?" Ali was hardly ever alone. He was usually in civic or business meetings, or with people who wanted something from him: advice, money or help. His curly, silver-streaked hair glistened in the moonlight, and his muscular body looked tight and tense. Only in his early forties, Ali looked much older from hard work and the stress of his success.

He answered in a faraway voice, "I was remembering my grandfather and his garden outside of the village. I loved working there as a boy. What would he think of Goreme now? What would he think of me?"

"He would be proud. You've built some of the best hotels in Cappadocia. You preserve the local environment and traditions. You employ many people and support others through your generosity. You have a beautiful family."

Ali lowered his eyes and whispered, "I don't know what's right or good anymore."

He resumed silently looking at the dark canyons. I'd known Ali for 15 years, and I knew we were done talking. I sat quietly, staring at the Tinker Bell lights shimmering in Goreme, which, from many previous visits, had become a second home to me.

Goreme is in the heart of Cappadocia, a moonscape covered with hundreds of phallic towers with tilting tips, mysterious arched caves, and conic tufa peaks called fairy chimneys. The fairy chimneys, a product of volcanic eruptions 10 million years ago, are unique sculptures chiseled by wind, rain and snow. Adorned with painted Byzantine stories and icons, some were used as churches. Variegated earth tone cliffs with rose-colored layers hide several underground cities that housed Christians seeking safety, first from the Romans and then from Turkish tribal regimes.

For centuries, the inhabitants of Cappadocia earned their living through subsistence farming. In 1985, UNESCO designated Goreme National Park and the Rock Sites of Cappadocia as a World Heritage Site, and since then it has become a tourist destination. Now, pictures of fairy chimneys and colorful hot air balloons floating in the sky above them feature on brochures and tourist websites about Turkey, and all the guidebooks say Goreme is a "must see" place.

At age 19, Ali had an arranged marriage and a year later a young daughter to support. As tourists came, he invited guests to sleep in his home. When more came, Ali put extra beds in his family cave home and, at his guests' insistence, charged a small amount of money. Demand exceeded the supply of rooms. Although he had never seen a hotel, through trial and error, he expanded his home and created the first cave hotel in Goreme.

Ali employed friends and neighbors. Local stonemasons melded each room into the structural integrity of the natural environment. Craftsmen created replicas of traditional Anatolian furniture, and village women embroidered bed linens and towels. Scouring Cappadocia for old urns, doors and farming tools, he placed them artistically around the hotel, reminders of the area's former agrarian way of life. He talked to old villagers to harvest Cappadocian history, becoming a steward of the area's traditions.

The morning after my chat with Ali, I walked to the village center. Shock assaulted me. Almost all of the cave homes had been replaced with hotels or restaurants. The old women who used to gather on the cobblestone path to gossip had all disappeared. No girls were weaving their dowry rugs outside their homes. The communal mill, once a busy meeting place, was now empty. Hammering and drilling sounds shattered the peace. Before, the most common noises were the clip-clop sound of donkey-led wagons and villagers' voices. Tourists and young locals sat in new cafes focused on their mobile devices drinking lattes instead of *cay*, Turkish tea, the lifeblood of Turkey.

I saw Ali on the main street. In a shaky voice with tears welling up, I asked, "Where are all the villagers? What's happened to Goreme?"

Ali explained that many had sold their cave homes for amounts of money they never could have imagined. Many built modern homes on the outskirts of town. They now worked in tourism—in the hotels, restaurants, hot air balloon companies and travel agencies—and made more money than they did from farming. "You can't blame them for wanting a better life," Ali said. "Goreme could not stay the way you remember it."

I wanted the villagers to have an easier life. But the traditional village I fell in love with was disappearing. Modernization was inevitable once Goreme opened up to tourism, but I just didn't realize it would happen so quickly.

Ali said, "I have decided to accept change in order to shape it."

A few days later, Ali picked me up in a jeep and took me to where his grandfather's garden had been. He was smiling and chatty, unlike the night on the terrace when melancholy shrouded him. We stopped at the edge of some ecru and rose cliffs overlooking a rock-filled valley. In good shape for a middle-aged man, Ali scampered down the side of the cliff, showering loose stones before him.

"I must hurry to pay some workers. Can you make it down yourself? At the bottom, just follow the path."

Not wanting to seem wimpy, I told him to go ahead. Soon I was perched on a narrow ledge frozen in place on the steep cliff. Climbing up and down cliffs must be part of the villagers' DNA in this land of peaks and valleys. Missing those chromosomes, I made the descent the best way I could, on my butt.

I followed a narrow path to a clearing surrounded by pockmarked cliff faces. From previous visits, I recognized these cavities as deserted pigeon houses. As a boy, Ali had cleaned pigeon houses, as pigeon poop had been a valuable commodity as a fertilizer. A man was judged worthy of marriage by the number of pigeon houses his family owned. If you were rich in pigeon poop, you were a good catch.

But pigeons disappeared after the appearance of commercial fertilizers about 30 years earlier. The garden was overgrown with dense brush, the fruit trees dormant and the vineyard fallow. Huge boulders had fallen, blocking the surrounding caves.

"I will make an organic garden here to honor the old ways," Ali announced, his dark eyes shining.

"Great," I said, forcing enthusiasm. I couldn't imagine how he could reincarnate the garden of his youth in this desolate valley.

I returned to Goreme two years later. Ali invited me to join hotel guests to make *pekmez*, a syrup made from grape juice thickened with mineral-filled local clay. It's the local cure-all, healing everything from the flu to a hangover. I accepted, but dreaded the climb down.

The next morning, a tractor coughing heavily crawled up the steep road towing a large, wooden ark-like contraption. We jumped on, and it chugged above the village through fairy chimneys and fields of yellow squash as Ali shared his memories of agrarian life in his grandfather's time. His passionate descriptions of the culture and community captivated us.

When we arrived at the spot where I slid down the cliff, I saw stone steps and a rope-railing. With a mischievous smile, Ali whispered, "I learned from your visit I had to build a path down to the garden. You won't need your ass." He didn't mean my donkey.

At the bottom of the cliff, we passed an orchard with trees drooping under the weight of blushing apples, chartreuse quince and purple figs. Rose bushes, geraniums and nasturtiums replaced the previously tangled overgrowth.

Two smiling, sun-baked women dressed in embroidered headscarves and patterned pantaloons stood over an oven carved into the rock. They were making *gozleme*, dough rolled very thin like a tortilla and baked over a wood-burning fire. A picnic table was set with a Turkish breakfast: boiled eggs (gathered from the chickens strutting around); locally made yogurt and cheeses; tomatoes, cucumbers, olives cured with local spices and garlic, all from Ali's garden. I heard echoes of cooing in the once barren complex of dovecotes. Ali had acquired 2,000 pigeons to produce organic fertilizer.

After breakfast, we hiked to harvest plump bunches of grapes. They were brought to another part of the garden where Ali had built a village house with a flat roof. In the past, I observed barefooted women pull up their pantaloons and dance on their rooftops stomping the grapes. We donned rubber boots, and while slipping and sliding on the rooftop, took turns crushing the grapes.

Lusty aromas of sizzling lamb and bulgur with tomato sauce called us back to the eating area. A local winemaker poured wine, which after a few glasses, might have rivaled the wines of Napa or Bordeaux.

Ali had hired a musician to serenade us on the *saz*, a traditional stringed instrument with a deep rounded back. With black hair and clothing, the musician looked like a Turkish Johnny Cash and sang soulful Turkish songs. Without noticing it, the day had slipped away. At its end, we piled into jeeps, having experienced a taste of traditional agrarian life in Cappadocia.

That night, I reflected on how complicated the impact of tourism on a community can be. Here it had brought prosperity to many and funded education and social services. Yet, tourism brought cultural change, increased traffic and strained the ecology of the area. Shifts in family life and friendships were occurring due to the 24/7 nature of tourism and competition for tourist dollars. Conscious efforts, such as Ali's, are needed to manage change and preserve traditions, the landscape and the other attributes that had made Goreme so appealing in the first place.

Keeping one foot in the past, another in the present, and his eyes on the future, Ali had found ways to balance preservation and progress. The making of *gozleme* and *pekmez*, the melodies of the *saz* floating through the canyons where pigeons now fly, all keep the collective memory alive.

Ali bounded up the stone steps and interrupted my thoughts. "Tomorrow night I am celebrating the full moon with a barbecue in the garden. Will you come?"

"I wouldn't miss it!" I replied smiling gratefully.

I think Ali's grandfather would be smiling too.

The Royal Mail Ship St. Helena departing for her namesake

A Royal Mail Ship—the End of an Era

Monica Conrady

I've always been intrigued by out-of-the-way, hard-to-reach places. I also love sea voyages. And that is how I found myself taking a ship with my Merchant Marine husband to the island of St. Helena in the South Atlantic, a British Overseas Territory, one of the most remote, populated places in the world. Until recently, ship was the only way to get there.

The ship in question was the RMS St. Helena, one of the last working Royal Mail Ships. The RMS sailed nearly 2,000 miles from Cape Town about once a month carrying cargo, supplies and just 128 passengers, some of whom were "Saints" as resident St. Helenians call themselves. From St. Helena it sails on to Ascension Island, another British Overseas Territory in the South Atlantic. From there, visitors can either sail back to Cape Town or fly on to England, to RAF Brize Norton, near Oxford, courtesy of the Royal Air Force. We chose the latter option.

It was early February when we arrived in Cape Town and made our way to the Mission for Seafarers at the port, the meeting place for those who would be traveling on the RMS. There we could change money, make phone calls, mail post cards, use the internet and have a snack before boarding a minibus to take us to the ship.

The RMS may be a working ship, but its passengers were well taken care of. Each day, the Ocean Mail, a paper outlining the day's events was delivered to everyone's cabin.

Breakfast, lunch, afternoon tea and dinner were served,

and there was a library, a fitness room and two lounges with well-stocked bars. Movies were shown and deck games arranged. But it was the chance to relax in a deck chair with a book as the shimmering blue Atlantic slipped by that appealed to me the most.

The fun started with the Captain's cocktail party, an occasion with a formal dress code, outlined in that morning's Ocean Mail. We were a relatively small group, so it was easy to get to know crew members and our fellow passengers.

After five days at sea, St. Helena was finally sighted. The tiny capital of Jamestown nestles dramatically in a v-shaped valley at the foot of towering cliffs. We anchored in James Bay and were taken ashore by launch. We stayed at one of the island's three hotels, the Wellington House, a Georgian building in the heart of town.

Along with some of our fellow passengers, we had booked a day's excursion with Corkers' Tours. Colin Corker picked us all up in his Charabanc, a 1929 open-air Chevy bus and away we went.

St. Helena's main claim to fame is that Napoleon was exiled here in 1815 after his defeat at the Battle of Waterloo. He died six years later. We visited the three main Napoleonic sites, the Briars Pavilion, Longwood House and Napoleon's tomb. His first stay on the island was at the Briars, where he spent a few weeks while his permanent residence at Longwood was being readied. He and his retinue found Longwood House to be a great disappointment, dark, damp and often surrounded by mist, altogether a far cry from the palaces of Napoleon's glory days. Later, we drove to Geranium Valley and Napoleon's first burial place. In 1840, nineteen years after his death, his coffin was unearthed and returned to France. Today, his remains lie in Les Invalides, in Paris.

We drove on to Plantation House, built in 1792 by the East India Company, now the residence of the island's Governor and home to Jonathan, a giant tortoise nearly 200 years old who lives in the grounds. We spotted neither.

Lastly, we went to the top of Jacobs Ladder, which stretches up from Jamestown to the top of Ladder Hill, 600 feet high with 699 steps. From there, we had a great view of Jamestown below.

Riding around in the Charabanc was great fun. We felt like school kids on an outing!

The next day we returned to the ship and set sail for Ascension Island, about 800 miles northeast. It was lovely to be back on board, lounging around, chatting with new friends, catching up on my reading. On our last night aboard, everyone got together for happy hour in the Sun Lounge followed by a farewell barbecue dinner on deck. We were sad to be leaving the ship.

At first, there didn't seem to be much of interest on Ascension Island. Georgetown, the island's capital and port, has just one place to stay, the Obsidian Hotel, formerly the official government guesthouse. Once settled in, we went for a stroll. Saint Mary's Church had an intriguing note on the door. "Welcome! This church is always open. Please shut the door to keep the donkeys out. Thank you." It sounded like a joke, until a couple of feral donkeys wandered over, looking for handouts!

With friends from the ship we hired a car and took off for the day. We visited Comfortless Cove, a pretty place with a sad history. In the 19th century, ships would drop off sailors stricken with the plague there. Islanders would then bring food and water and leave it for them to prevent an epidemic spreading in their own community. Apparently when the food was left untouched, they knew the last sailor had died.

At the end of the 19th century, the first transatlantic telegraph cables were brought ashore at this point. The relay cable house for the service can still be seen today.

We then headed up to the Green Mountain area. As we climbed, the arid landscape below gave way to lush greenery. It felt like being in a rainforest.

Back in Georgetown, it seemed everyone in town gathers at the hotel bar to socialize and tell of the day's happenings.

It was a good day, but the best was yet to come.

Between January and May, giant green turtles migrate from Brazil to Ascension Island to breed. Although several beaches on the island are nesting grounds, the largest and most accessible is Long Beach, about a 10-minute walk from the hotel.

After engaging in offshore courting and mating, the females make their way up the beach and dig deep nests. They then lay around 100 soft, white eggs and cover them up. Having laid their eggs, they make their way back to the sea.

Late that night, we walked over to the beach, moving slowly and being very careful where we shone our flashlights. We could hear the sound of their flippers digging and pushing the sand around. It was an unforgettable experience. We then went back again at dawn. They had gone—all that remained were their tracks down the beach to the sea. That is, except for one poor turtle who was still frantically trying to finish burying her eggs. I almost felt like jumping down and helping her.

Time to leave. That afternoon we were transported out to Wideawake Airfield for our flight to the U.K. The name comes from a noisy colony of birds—sooty terns—nicknamed wideawakes from the sound of their distinctive call.

I was expecting an RAF plane to be something rough and ready, but it turned out to be a charter plane from a major airline—very comfortable with excellent food and drink, plus we were all lent an iPad to watch movies. Who would have guessed?

After landing at Brize Norton we were met by an old friend who lived nearby and whisked us away.

Visiting those two isolated islands in the South Atlantic was one of the most memorable trips we have ever taken. With a long-awaited airport now open on St. Helena, the Royal Mail Ship is no more. It is, indeed, the end of an era.

Churchyard in Ballyvaughn, Western Ireland

Searching for My Irish Roots, Finding Myself

Diane Covington-Carter

As far back as I can remember, I knew I was Irish.

My mother talked about how her ancestors left Ireland in 1852, setting off across the ocean to a new life in Melbourne, Australia. Her grandfather was five.

When my mother spoke of her grandfather, she called him her *Irish* grandfather, not her Australian grandfather. She always used his full name in these stories, *Michael Thomas Gleeson*, and the awe in her voice told how much she respected and loved him.

For a special treat, I'd be allowed to play my mother's Kate Smith record on my small record player. I'd lean in close, humming along with the songs: "Molly Malone," which seemed so sad, "My Wild Irish Rose" and "When Irish Eyes are Smiling," my favorite.

As the years passed, I'd read about genealogy websites and wonder—was it possible to trace our Irish roots?

A year before my mother died, I was planning a trip to Ireland and wanted to do some sleuthing into our family tree. I discovered that if we ordered a copy of my great-grandfather's death certificate from Australia, it would list where he had been born in Ireland.

When we discovered the name of his village, Gowran, in Kilkenny County, I stayed up late searching for more information and came across a site called "Kilkenny Family Names

Search." On it, I found a Brian Gleeson, from Melbourne, Australia. I typed out a quick email.

The next morning, when I opened my email, his name jumped out at me. Yes, he knew of my great-grandfather: Brian's great-grandfather and mine had been cousins. But then I almost fell off my chair. Brian was completing a 500-page book about the Gleeson family tree and had made many trips to Ireland to research it.

I couldn't believe my good luck. As we emailed back and forth, he gave me all the important facts and places to go.

A month later, as my Aer Lingus flight circled, I marveled at the lush, green landscape, surrounded by the sparkling blue ocean. Once past customs, I got into my tiny rental car, trying to get used to being on the other side of the front seat, and to remember to drive on the other side of the road. I took a deep breath, followed the car in front of me and headed in the general direction of Kilkenny County and Gowran.

That afternoon, I found a B&B and the proprietor nodded when I told her I was looking for my family roots. In the nearby town, a bowl of thick soup, served with warm soda bread and rich butter, made the perfect supper. I snapped photos of signs for Gleeson Realty, Gleeson Bar and Gleeson Brothers Company, reveling in the novelty of seeing our family name.

It was odd how at home I felt. Everyone greeted me warmly and someone even stopped me on the street, mistaking me for a friend. I did seem to look like everyone else: Wow, I *am* Irish!

The next morning, a Sunday, I found my way to the small village of Gowran. I arrived at the church during Mass, so slipped into a pew in the back. I sat in awe and thought—*This is the same place where my great-grandfather went to church, before they left for Australia.* It was my first experience of knowing that I was linked back in time, over 150 years, to a place I'd never been before. I had roots here.

After the Mass, I followed the white-haired priest to the vestry to look through the church records. It took him a few moments to find the right box for 1847, but then he handed me a leather-bound book.

Within a few minutes of squinting at faded handwriting, I found my great-grandfather's baptismal record. His parents had signed it, so with their names I located their marriage records a year before. *Bridget Maher had married John Gleeson, right near where I sat. My great-great grandparents. If they hadn't gotten married, I would not be sitting here.*

I couldn't have explained the jolt of energy that tingled through me when I spotted their names. Or why it moved me to look at the handwriting on the yellowed pages that had been so carefully preserved.

I sat for a while, just staring at their names.

What had it been like to leave their home and travel across the world to a new country?

But the letters on the page gave me no new answers.

As I left the village, I rolled down the car windows and let in the spring breeze, listening to a radio station from Dublin.

The narrow road wound past green farm fields, villages with church steeples and lines of fresh laundry flapping in the breeze. As I was going over the wonder of the day, Bruce Springsteen came on the radio singing "Born in the USA." I turned it up, singing along with his raspy voice, belting out the words.

Yeah, *I was born in the USA.*

That was the truth. I am American.

But all those relatives in the church directory, who voyaged so far to make a new life, they would be proud of me, exactly as I am: a Yank who cared about her Irish roots enough to travel back to Ireland to see their names in the parish registry.

Yeah, *I was born in the USA,* I thought.

But down deep, I'm Irish.

Black Mountain Valley

Black Mountain Valley, China's Enchanted Oasis

Lee Daley

On a cool October morning, I traveled by bus from the port city of Chongqing to Black Mountain Valley, a place of untamed raw beauty full of mystery, lush vegetation and silver-hued waterfalls. The two-hour excursion on a narrow two-lane road through greenery-covered mountains delivered me from one world—of airports, highways and cruise ships—to another amidst nature's unplanned majesty. It felt like an act of purification.

Fall color blessed our little group with blazing orange and red maples hovering over a cascading stream at the valley's entry. Like a row of line dancers, each of us stretched out our arms, carefully navigating the narrow rock path across the stream. Chasing moments and selfies, we soon diverged into twosomes and solos to explore the valley's vistas of deep canyons, majestic karsts and magnificent waterfalls.

Black Mountain Valley contains more than 1,800 varieties of plants in an enclave of 97-percent virgin forest with densely wooded slopes and sun-dappled valleys. The hike (about eight miles) passes through two narrow valleys with easily navigable planked walkways built above the streams. Stupendous views of towering karsts excite the eye. Fog formations circle the peaks while mischievously merging with a myriad of waterfalls. At the beginning of the hike, the stream cascades downhill until the valley levels; then one can view the falls on the distant horizon as they rush toward the valley's low spot. Wide panoramas narrow to arm's width at one juncture where it becomes possible to reach out and almost touch both of the canyon walls. The widest passageway can be up to 90 feet while the narrowest is less than six feet.

At one spot, I lingered near a fast-flowing stream, taking in its tumultuous energy, wanting to memorize the moment. Red ribbons, draped on an overhanging branch, floated on a breeze. The rush of water, a bird's call and my calm breath as I planted my feet at the water's edge were the only audible sounds. Through the trees, I could make out karsts, each hundreds of feet tall. Fog billowed and circled the peaks in a celestial caress. As if on cue, a cinematic sunbeam spotlighted the scene. For a moment, I was one small entity in an infinite world of harmony. Feeling a serenity I could inhabit forever, I reached for my camera hoping to capture the magic.

We often spied red ribbons festooned from trees and arbors along the path. In Chinese culture, the color red symbolizes good luck and joy. Buddhists believe that tying a red ribbon to a "wishing tree" will make your wish come true, that forces from the heavens will hear the wish. The higher the ribbon, the more likely the wish will be heard.

So, if your travels take you to China, remember to make a wish and tie a red ribbon on a "wishing tree." Fact, fiction or fantasy, I love the concept.

Waterfalls became more abundant as we made our way through the valley. Where the path narrowed, the stream became a river that we carefully traversed on a shaking rope bridge. We then followed a cliffside trail to rejoin the original walkway. I had to remind myself to watch where I stepped as I was so taken by the terrain, the towering cliffs streaked with white limestone deposits, the trickling springs, natural fountains and lush green forest. It was a primitive, pristine scene. Such beauty is rarely encountered this close to a city, especially one the size of Chongqing with its 9 million inhabitants.

As one of the country's best-preserved natural scenic areas, native naturalists refer to Black Mountain Valley as the nation's wildlife genome bank. China rates the preserve a 5A tourist site, the same status as The Great Wall.

The last leg of our hike was the most challenging but ultimately the most rewarding. Here, we encountered a steep uphill climb with more than a mile of steps built into the terrain. As dusk fell, only a handful of walkers remained. Many had chosen to ride the cable car offered before the stairway trek. But beauty seduced us. Up and up we trudged. It was now so humid that, as we climbed, the air seemed to part around us.

Our original group of eight had dwindled to three. With my spouse and one other hiker, we would most likely be the last to reach the parking area outside the forest. But we were not alone. I noticed a park ranger holding up the rear and felt relieved to see that the forest service was protecting us.

Our other companion was a slow walker due to an old knee injury. I didn't know Susan well but was amazed at her pluck. We had both passed and trailed her many times during the day. While John and I lingered, savoring the sights, capturing photos, Susan kept to the planked walkway–slow but steady–taking her own measure of the magic. We noticed her pace had slowed even more. Not the time for decorum. John and I decided it was best to wait and make our way out together.

Just as we were sure we couldn't face another steep stairway, the three of us reached a wide landing. Above us. a massive outcropping loomed. From its peak, a silvery veil of water flowed. Following its roar, we peered over the rail to where a pristine crystal lagoon lay spread before us. Dozens of shimmering orange carp swirled and dove beneath the currents. Resembling a string of pearls, water droplets rose and fell. It was an ethereal scene straight out of Shangri-la. Black Mountain seemed to know we had earned this reward.

Soon, we were almost there. At the end of the trail. Time to say goodbye to Black Mountain Valley, a bittersweet moment. I looked back at the stone cathedrals with a sense of awe and gratitude. After spending so much time admiring them, the waterfalls had become my neighbors, almost my friends. With a sigh, I whispered goodbye.

As we stood at the brink of a steep stairway overlooking the parking pad, we realized the stairway's narrow steps were built without a handrail. Nestling Susan between us, we linked arms and slowly proceeded. It was then I realized that when you spend a day in the mountains together, you become more than neighbors and fellow hikers. You become friends.

Life on Peru's upper Amazon revolves around food, and it doesn't get any fresher than this just-caught caiman.

Amazon Calm: Exploring the Good Life off the Grid

Ginger Dingus

The barefoot fisherman, weathered and sun-browned, silently paddled his dugout canoe up to our drifting motorboat. He carried a handmade spear, two fishing poles cut from twigs and a well-worn rifle. To him, it was just another day's hunt for groceries—fresh fish, wild pig, maybe even a capybara, the Amazon rain-forest's dog-sized rodent. The capybara is the world's largest rat and, according to our knowledgeable Peruvian guide, George Davila, it makes a tasty meal.

"Can you imagine people still live like this?" Michael Barth, an intrepid traveler from Switzerland, shook his head in disbelief.

We, 11 American and European adventure seekers on a weeklong riverboat journey on Peru's remote upper Amazon River, felt equally amazed. Easy for us to pop open our picnic baskets and tuck into a breakfast of ham and cheese sandwiches, tangerines and piping hot coffee. Little did we realize that we would soon be using sticks and string to catch our own dinner—a meal of fresh, feisty piranhas.

It was 7:30 on a sunny, humid, not yet too-hot April morning. Already we were an hour into the day's first motorboat safari, heading deeper into the jungle than our 125-foot riverboat could navigate. So far, we had chanced upon four species of monkeys and a three-toed sloth hanging out in the branches of a mimosa tree. Among the hundreds of birds whirling overhead, George identified scarlet macaws, white-throated toucans, bright green parakeets, various hawks and a yellow-rumped cacique, a.k.a. "butter butt."

We handed the lone fisherman a couple of sandwiches and packets of juice. In exchange, he showed us how he threw his spear to catch fish. We watched him paddle away as we polished off breakfast.

An hour later, we cruised past four happy hunters busily chopping up a freshly caught caiman (small crocodile) on the muddy riverbank. The men eagerly held up their prize for photos. The tail was missing, so they jokingly put it back on the gutted body. One man pulled open the caiman's toothy jaw, inserted his arm and pretended he was being attacked. Another used sign language to show us the bait, a large hook hidden inside a catfish. Only the chewed fish head remained.

Even today, life on the Amazon, at least on this isolated part of the river, is a far cry from the concrete jungle. There's no running water. No cars. No cell phones. Electricity is by generator, if at all. Pocket money comes from selling plantains to a middleman and handicrafts to the occasional tourist.

Surprisingly, meeting villagers living off the grid proved as fascinating as seeing the spectacularly colored birds and jungle wildlife that originally attracted most of us to the trip.

Our riverboat odyssey began in Iquitos, in northeastern Peru. The once-booming rubber-producing town can only be reached by air (we flew in from Lima) or by boat. At 2,300 miles from the mouth of the Amazon on the Atlantic Ocean, it's the world's most inland seaport. From Iquitos, our riverboat headed another 300 miles upriver on the Amazon, Ucayali and Maranon rivers, far off the beaten tourist path.

I traveled on the 31-passenger La Amatista (which means

amethyst), a riverboat built locally of native woods and designed to look like a houseboat owned by a 19th-century rubber baron. Think "African Queen," and you'll get the idea. Thankfully the cabins, though small, featured air-conditioning and private bathrooms with hot shower water filtered from the Amazon. (There was plenty of bottled water to drink.) Meals were casual buffets in a dining room with a view. The menu featured such local foods as catfish, Peruvian potatoes stuffed with tuna, chicken, rice, plenty of fresh veggies and luscious tropical fruits.

Our days typically began with breakfast around 7 a.m., followed immediately by a motorboat ride on the river or small creek in search of rain-forest wildlife. We were back aboard around 11 a.m., in time for a nature lesson before lunch. Who knew the Amazon discharges as much water in two hours as New York City uses in a year?

During the hot midday hours (the area lies about four degrees south of the Equator), we enjoyed siestas. We climbed back in the motorboat around 4 p.m. for more critter encounters or to visit primitive villages. Civilized cruising began at sunset with cocktails on the upper deck. Dinner and a stargazing or caiman-hunting boat ride in the dark rounded out the day.

On a particularly memorable outing one eerily quiet night, I discovered one of the Amazon's most striking and least promoted marvels. Hundreds of thousands of sparkling stars lit up the sky in the most spectacular light show I have ever witnessed. What we in the West call the dark sky was ablaze. On every trip since, I've been searching for one more glimpse of that incredible dark sky.

Night or day, on each excursion, George, who grew up

on the Amazon, made a new discovery—green iguanas sunning in the trees, a troop of 50-plus squirrel monkeys toting babies on their backs, a family of bug-eyed nocturnal owl monkeys peeking from a hole in a tall tree, a slow-moving sloth, pink dolphins, giant lily pads, blue morpho butterflies and exotic birds by the hundreds. His technique? He listened to the jungle telegraph and could recognize individual voices. To us, chattering monkeys sounded like screeching parrots.

One afternoon, George found a fishing hole by watching vultures perched in overhead branches. He was right on. The instant we dropped our beef-baited hooks into the muddy, cocoa-brown river, the piranhas started biting. In 20 minutes, we caught a feast of 46 fish. One overeager fellow traveler got an unexpected souvenir. Instead of letting the guide unhook his catch, he learned the painful way that fingers make easy targets for a piranha's razor-sharp teeth. At dinner, the rest of us discovered piranhas are bony little devils and a lot of trouble to eat.

The river people or "*riberenos*" were a constant source of wonder. Curious children ran to meet us as we cruised to their remote villages. They giggled at our digital photos, picked flowers for the ladies and eagerly recited their lessons when we visited their rustic schools. The adults proudly showed off their one-room, thatched-roof huts built by hand and resting atop stilts as protection from seasonal flooding.

"They get everything they need from nature," George commented. "Water, food, houses." Nature even supplies free transport in the form of wood to make dugout canoes and paddles.

"Maybe they've got a better life than we do," Michael mused.

Maybe, but I'll stick with the riverboat's creature comforts while exploring the Amazon. Just bring on the stars. I'm ready to be dazzled.

Istanbul rug merchants spreading a rug to sell

Buying a Rug

M.T. Eley

In times of panic and nationwide unease, like, say, 2020, it is imperative to remember that there are essential businesses of humanity that once concerned us and will concern us again, such as avoiding rug-buying. To forget them, in the slurry of the live stream of consciousness that our public sphere has become, would be foolish; we would be led like sheep to the slaughter at the hands of conniving Turkish rug merchants, much as I was some years ago in Istanbul.

There is an art to emerging as a traveler from a visit to the Bosporus without a rug, and I had not learned it at the time. Perhaps it cannot be done, or at least done by a first-time visitor, and this explains the continued success of the Turkish economy at a time when little else is going for the country. It is a side effect of the larger spell cast upon you as soon as you inhale that ancient air, and this is not simply tourist-office copywriting.

Istanbul is sometimes described as enchanted, which is too sugary a word for the darker sense of bewitchment one has in the city, walking in the permanent shadows from the West and the breezes wafting off the great straits. You have at once the cool chill of classical antiquity and the wild fantasia of the Orient, bound up in spices and colors and murmurs and calls to prayer; ancient forces, tugging at each other like the currents in the Bosporus. As a Westerner, there is a sense of having once belonged here but no more; whispers of both dying Rome and millennia before, burning Troy whose ruins rest further down the waters. Wrapped around and steeped in such a place are a thousand cobbled streets, and stores in imitation of Europe, and bazaars in proud imitation of nobody, and mosques all alike yet none identical, and basements full of Turkish rugs.

I had set out hours before my flight out from the old Ataturk Airport with a stomach full of the oil-fried breakfast served by the bed and breakfast. My aim was simple: to find a book of international stamps for a bevy of postcards to send back home. Stamps are more easily bought abroad than they are in the United States; every store has a book somewhere, sometimes from a previous decade but nonetheless enough to make it past the mail scanners and into the mail bins. But like a rube I turned into a shop which advertised, besides a rusting rack of "*postcartes*", international stamps for sale.

"I'd like to buy stamps," I announced, signing my death warrant.

"Ah, yes, stamps! We have those in the back," said the shopkeeper, stepping with zeal from behind his counter and waving off a nameless shopgirl to fetch my undoing. A more experienced traveler would have fled; I remained, an un-traveled young American who believed human baseness did not extend beyond tipping in one dollar bills. How much would those be? I inquired. The answer was not forthcoming, but hot apple tea was served in its place.

The servant girl—something I do not say casually, but in earnest, for she did not have any other role in this frowsty den—whisked in with a silver platter bearing two glasses of apple tea. The fusion of dried apple slices and rose hips, slightly stronger than apple juice but considerably weaker than tea or cider, steamed in clouds in the cool outdoor air in slender, tulip-like glasses. Noticing the tea's discomfort at the cold, the shopkeeper invited me in, or rather down a set of stairs. I reminded him of the stamps.

"Ah, yes, the stamps are right by the apple tea." The servant girl, snapped at in Turkish for her foolishness in confusing the two, was dispatched. "But in the meantime, please come down from the cold! Please tell me—have you ever purchased a Turkish rug?" I began to suspect that the shop had never had stamps, had never intended to have stamps, and that the girl had been sent off to another store, probably on the other side of the Bosporus and with inexact change.

But somehow, and perhaps by magic, I found myself sitting down on an immense pile of rugs, which coughed with centuries-old dust as I perched atop them, the dust clouds illuminated by a few wall light fixtures of octogenarian status. We were surrounded by even higher piles, which, like sedimentary rock, threatened to become one solid mass, to be mined centuries hence as a sustainable building material. The merchant sipped his tea.

"Friend, my family has long worked in the rug trade in these distant mountains. They are too poor to come here, but I have been here for many years, and I journey back often with these rugs, made of finest cotton. If only the Americans *knew* of these rugs' pedigree"—the word was a practiced one—"they would buy only from me. These are all loomed by hand, evaluated by hand, finished by hand. All by hand."

I mentioned the stamps and was dismissed much like the servant girl who was, I hoped, fleeing for her life. The merchant peeled an immense rug off a convenient pile, its design admittedly intricate. I confessed appreciation.

"Ah, you see! You see. Five thousand lira for this in the Grand Bazaar." I computed in the back of my mind and was relieved that $750 was too absurd a price to be extracted from me, sympathy for the man's family or not. "But here, because you have honored me by coming here, I will gladly say 500 lira."

Outwitted, I struggled for a likely excuse, finding one in my backpack and sole piece of luggage. "I traveled economy," I explained. "Aegean Airlines would never allow that to come onboard, it's far too big and the luggage charge would easily cost its price. But I will gladly take the stamps."

"A curse upon the Greeks!" thundered the merchant. "I have relatives in Turkish Airlines and they would have let you fly free bearing such an article." I did not doubt it—many members of this man's family seemed driven to menial labor due to international ignorance of their rugs' value. "However, it is not just you leave Turkey without one of our rugs. Allah forbid!" He cast his eyes on my backpack and found inspiration. "Ah!" Disappearing behind another stack, he reappeared with a much smaller rug—more of a mat—in a queer sort of mustard yellow with black motifs. I wished to say it was revolting except I feared it was a prayer rug and Allah had been invoked already.

"This is a traditional couples' mat," he began. It was hardly mat enough for a single person, much less two, but I did not press the point. "Four hundred lira for so priceless an item, for so beautiful a couple as you will surely be a part of someday. It will bless the marriage." He gazed into my eyes with utter sincerity. I felt villainous and imagined the distant cousins stitching the abomination together, weaving wedding well-wishes into the woof. Sixty-one dollars was still too much for a charmed carpet, though; I shook my head and made a movement to go.

"Three hundred!" he pleaded. A blow was dealt. Three hundred lira lurked in my pocket, with hours remaining to spend it. But I did not want the article. I said as much.

"Two hundred is a steal," the merchant fumed. "It barely covers the cost of the tea or my hospitality." (I did not mention the stamps.) But his being irked was the wrong strategy, and I felt emboldened by his taking offense. I rose and took up my backpack. Outside, the mosques, all 10 thousand of them, began the call to prayer, the mournful *ezan* filling the air with overworked megaphone intonations. The merchant saw his error and placed the mat down and kneeled upon it.

"Allah," he said in the decent English that I assume he made his regular supplications in, "Thank you for this guest. Thank you his blessing, his home, his home. One hundred lira and it is his, is destined to be his, is bound to be his and you have ordained it."

A rustling was heard up the stairs.

I walked out of the shop minutes later, 100 lira poorer, with two international stamps. Seven dollars apiece is not too bad a price to send a postcard hurtling across the world. And it is not too bad a price for a Turkish rug you do not want.

A typical Philippine bus offering free air conditioning on the roof,
and by removing the windshield

Keeping Cool in the Philippines

Bill Fink

I refused to yield to the knuckle in my back. The man behind me had a death grip on the metal frame atop my bus seat. His knuckles angled so that whenever I tried to relax, they ground directly in my spine. Each of the hundreds of times the bus hit a rut in the Philippine road, the sharp jabbing hand poked me. And we were only two hours into the eight-hour trip from Manila to Banaue.

Exhaust seeped through the cracked windows. Dust coated my teeth in a gritty paste. Sweat mixed with the grime covering my face to create a muddy run-off onto my already filthy shirt. My day had been one long battle with both the elements and my fellow travelers. I was in no mood for compromise so I pushed back, hard, into his hand.

My trip was to the "Eighth Natural Wonder of the World," the rice terraces of Banaue in the mountains of northern Luzon Island. I planned to relax in this rural retreat, hiking through hills covered with endless seas of rice plants waving in cool mountain breezes.

At the central Manila bus terminal, wheezing buses spewed diesel fumes into the sweltering heat and humidity of the city. By the time I fought my way through a mob of a line to buy a ticket and find the bus, my spit was black from the pollution, and my backpack made me feel as if a 30-pound leech was stuck on my shoulders, sucking out my lifeblood.

To save money, I was riding low-grade Philippine public transport: a vintage 1970s orange school bus which looked as though it had been handed down from a series of increasingly impoverished third-world countries. People shoved their way aboard through a departing crowd dragging bundles, boxes and babies. When I entered, every seat already had at least two people in it. Most of the filthy windows were stuck closed, and the few which were open a crack brought no fresh air. The passengers' agitation stewed the stale, stagnant air of the bus into a soup of misery.

When I tried to wedge myself into a small space in the middle of a group in the back of the bus, they erupted in a flurry of hissing, muttering and spitting, causing me to flee for a better position.

I pushed my way to the mid-bus exit door, or at least where the door would have been had it not been torn out in some long-forgotten accident. I hoped to sit on the steps, perhaps catching a breeze once the bus hit the road. But people continued to push aboard, each one trying to knock me from this prized location.

The last man to enter stood in the doorway to force me inward. Climbing up a step, I was then too tall to stand erect under the low ceiling. I did not want to spend eight hours hunched into a question-mark shape, so I gave up the stoop. If I had stayed, I might have ended the trip like a crooked old farmer bent permanently from a lifetime in the rice fields.

I managed to squeeze onto the edge of a seat filled with two small but surly villagers. Once the bus started, they seemed to use every bounce as an opportunity to slide me off of the seat into the aisle. And then, about 45 minutes into the ride, the man behind me started the knuckle treatment.

The views served as a distraction, as Manila's cityscape

devolved from skyscrapers to suburbs to shantytowns, and then to tropical jungle as we headed north. Clapboard wooden *sari-sari* shacks selling Pop Cola and Granny Goose chips dotted the side of the road like mile-markers.

As the hours went by, the oppressive heat in the bus felt more than just muggy, it was like a mugging. I wilted in my seat, but the knuckles jabbed me back to attention. I was tired of giving in to the elements and to the pushy people around me.

So I neither moved to the side nor leaned forward to avoid the knuckles, deciding to fight and win this bus ride competition of discomfort, pressing backward with all my weight hoping the man's hand would be crushed. Surely he'd have to move it soon? Another hour passed without either of us giving an inch. The tough, gnarled knuckles in my back had probably been hardened by decades of working dusty Philippine fields.

As if the heat and noise and bumping weren't enough, a foul odor began to fill the air. The baby in the seat in front of me had been screaming most of the trip, and had now soiled himself. The mother simply removed the cloth diaper, and shook it out of the window.

The contents of the diaper caught in the slipstream of the bus and flew directly in the face of the man who had taken my spot in the open doorway. His shrieks of disgust and howls of anger flew back at the woman like verbal human waste. The woman yelled in response. The baby screamed. The people around them argued in a confusion of dialects, shouting even louder when others didn't understand.

Amidst the furious yelling across the bus, it was time to

try a new strategy. I turned to politely ask the man in the seat behind me if he would mind removing his knuckles from my back. "*No problema,*" he replied. He calmly folded his giant, gnarled hands into his lap. He probably hadn't even noticed my weight in the prior hours.

"Banaue?" he asked. I nodded.

Amidst all the shouting, the bouncing and the heat, he smiled at me like a dusty Buddha.

"*Maganda* (It's beautiful)," he said.

I wasn't completely sure if he was referring to the views, our destination or, somehow, the bus ride. So, like him, I leaned back, folded my hands and smiled. Despite the high temperature, the Philippines then became a little bit cooler for me.

Marketplace in the town of Ranomafana

Speaking Malagasy

Laurie McAndish King

She's as tattered a child as I've ever seen, wrapped—even in the tropical heat—in ragged layers I can hardly identify as clothing. Her bare feet are covered in dust and seem to grow out of the ground as she stands frozen, eyeing me from the edge of the road. Behind the girl the jungle rises up, green and dense. Between the girl and the jungle is what must be her home—a one-room shack, built with scraps of wood and covered with rusty pieces of corrugated tin. A blue plastic bucket sits near the opening that serves as a doorway. I've seen many such houses here in Madagascar.

"*Salama.* Hello." I stand in the middle of the wide dirt road, smiling hopefully at the little girl and calling out the only Malagasy word I can remember. My left hand shades my face from the summer sun.

No response.

I'm in Madagascar to study the environmental needs of lemurs, but it's the Malagasy people who really affect me. Most of them live in extreme poverty. I've already learned to say *tsy misy,* "there isn't any," to the flocks of children begging in the streets. They press eagerly against my body, but I don't feel threatened like I would in almost any other country. These children are gentle. They ask for a *stilo*—a pen—although they rarely attend school and can't afford paper to write on. Even after it's clear I have no *stilos* to offer, three girls reach out and touch my arm softly, feeling the fabric of my shirtsleeve. The shyer kids smile from a distance, studying my light skin and hair.

All the other researchers speak English, so there was technically no need for me to learn the local language. Which is a good thing, because I find even a simple sentence—such as, "Excuse me, where is the market?" *(Aiza no misy ny tsena, aza fady?)*—impossible to spit out, let alone to replicate in the melodic tones of the Malagasy language. "It is still difficult for me to understand what people say," translates to *Mbola sarota amiko ny mahazo izay lazain'ny olona.* I am conversationally challenged, to say the least.

One bright Saturday morning I walk from camp into town. That's when I meet the little girl. She can't be more than five or six years old, yet she is completely alone. Her arms are full of green-leafed branches, which she's carrying down the hill, probably into Ranomafana town for her mother to sell at the market.

The girl still has more than a mile to go, and, since the market is my destination as well, I hope to share the walk with her.

"*Salama.*" I say hello again.

Now I regret that I didn't bother to learn more of the language. I say my name and point to myself, then point to the girl, asking her name in English. Of course she doesn't speak my language, but maybe she will understand my pantomime. The girl studies me, then slowly extends the armful of wild herbs she is carrying, even though we stand more than 30 feet apart. I take a step toward her; she backs quickly into the jungle. I give up and head down the road. But then the girl begins to follow me, keeping her distance, yet eager to interact. Her dark eyes sparkle with anticipation.

Madagascar is like that child. It is a young country, hopeful and poor. It is so remote as to be almost wild. And it is slipping into the sea. Overcrowding has led to extreme erosion, and torrential rains wash dirt down the mountain slopes, driving nutrients through gullies, into rivers and out to sea. Viewed from the air, Madagascar bleeds, its red earth streaming a hundred miles into the Indian Ocean.

In spite of this environmental tragedy, the Malagasy people are hopeful and resilient. They are well known for enjoying music, poetry and witty proverbs. ("Other people's children cause your nostrils to flare" is my favorite, so far.) Eloquence is such an important part of life that, according to folklore, "It is the master of the words who rules the kingdom."

I cannot master these words. Not only that, but my what's-your-name pantomime has failed to get through to the little girl. Five minutes into our interaction, *salama* no longer seems appropriate.

So I resort to whistling. I begin with something easy— the first three notes from the "Close Encounters of the Third Kind" theme song.

She whistles back! Then she gives a little jump of joy.

I try a longer sequence, all five notes, and the girl puckers up and responds in perfect pitch. Then she whistles her own melody, and I do my best to mimic her tune in reply. She's a much better musician than I am. Finally the girl approaches, extending her thin arms and thrusting the herbs toward me.

I reach out and rub a small leaf between my thumb and forefinger, then sniff it, hoping both to connect with the girl and to identify the herb. But the scent, like the language, is completely foreign. I can only smile appreciatively.

That is enough. The girl becomes my wary companion, skipping alongside me, always at arm's length, whistling her tunes and mine, and finally, just outside of town, singing me a lovely song in her small, faraway voice. As soon as we reach the bustling marketplace she slips into the sea of faces, leaving me to wander, scanning the crowd for her shy smile, straining to hear a song or a whistle. I search for more than an hour, but never see her again.

I think a lot about the Malagasy people during these COVID-19 days, when we are adjusting to living without "non-essential services" and other things we took for granted just a few months ago. We are learning now what the Malagasy people already know—the significance of a gesture of friendship, the importance of music, how to appreciate what we have. Sometimes I whistle the first five notes of "Close Encounters" to myself as a reminder of the little Malagasy girl. I never learned her name, but she spoke to me in a profound way—without ever saying a word.

Pronghorn, sometimes called California Antelope

Carrizo Gold: Nature's Hardest Hue to Hold

David Laws

I pulled my jacket close against the chill stirring of an early breeze. A heavy silence enveloped the world in the final, darkest minutes before dawn. To the east, a gray sliver of pending morning peeked from beneath bands of straggling clouds to silhouette the rugged crest of the Temblor Range. Planning a day exploring the Carrizo Plain, I had risen early to watch the sunrise from this elevated spot at the northern entrance to the national monument, about 70 miles east of San Luis Obispo, that has been called "California's Serengeti."

From my vantage point on the promontory of Soda Lake Overlook, white mineral deposits bordering the water reflected a swelling glow in the east, the first sign of physical landscape in an ocean of darkness. Orange tints, brightening by the minute, injected a promise of color into the neutral gray of the fading night. As the spectrum moved to the red of blood, ragged peaks sharply etched against the horizon slowly, slowly released the tip of a glowing disk. The first rays of sunlight spilled out over the ridgeline into morning.

A newborn flash of green-gold light, immortalized by poet Robert Frost as "nature's hardest hue to hold," dissolved into pinks and yellows and reds and blues against the disparate textures of rocks, sand, scrub, saline wetlands and wildflowers. Denizens of the Plain, from blunt-nosed leopard lizards, pronghorn and giant tule elk, and burrowing owls to high-flying ferruginous hawks, began their scurrying and soaring.

With typical annual rainfall of fewer than 10 inches, Carrizo qualifies as desert country. Not the slickrock Utah desert of Edward Abbey or the endless crescent dunes of T. E. Lawrence's Arabia, but a grassland with wildlife and vegetation more typical of a prairie. Isolated from the coast on the west and the great Central Valley to the east by mountain-building earthquake movements along the San Andreas Fault, the 50-mile-long by 10-mile-wide flat plain was sacred to the Chumash people for thousands of years. They called it "the place of the rabbits."

Established in 2001 as the Carrizo Plain National Monument, nearly 250,000 acres between the Temblor and Caliente mountain ranges are preserved as public lands. Volunteers are gradually removing fencing and structures from recent ranching activity to return the valley to a landscape that has changed little in thousands of years, except for violent lurches to the north every century or so.

Lingering shadows dissolved in the flood of daylight, revealing a slope of orange-tinged fiddleneck blooms. A rising song of western meadowlarks broke the silence. Hailed as the essential musical theme of the American West prairie lands, their melodious refrain accompanied my walk downhill to a boardwalk edging Soda Lake.

Rainfall once drained into the Salinas River but is now trapped in the shallow basin of the Plain. Covering 3,000 acres when full, Soda Lake is the largest remaining natural alkali wetland in Southern California. With no outlet, summer evaporation leaves a vast expanse of white mineral salts that shimmer and sway in the afternoon heat. Early settlers mined these saline deposits for preserving meat. Sandy spots alongside the walk glowed with California goldfields. The intense yellow carpet flowed like liquid gold between gray skeletons of the last season's spiny saltbush shrubs. Eager to arrive on time for a coveted spot on a guided tour of Painted Rock, the dominant cultural feature of the Plain, I hastened back to my car.

Seasonal intern Gannon gathered our group outside the Goodwin Education and Visitor Center. He pointed to our destination, Painted Rock, a sandstone outcrop protruding through the level valley floor that served as a sacred meeting place of the Chumash, Salinan and Yokut people for generations. Access is restricted to preserve ancient pictographs and to protect nesting falcons and other raptors.

We entered an open horseshoe-shaped area at the center of the rock. Painted on the walls of eroded caves along the base, pictographs in multiple layers of black, red and white pigment from charcoal and local minerals span a period estimated from 3,000 to just 200 years ago. Images of animals and humans, together with abstract representations of water, fertility, rain and religious symbols, survived centuries of weathering. Modern vandals have not been so kind. Carved graffiti and shotgun blasts have taken their toll.

I tried to imagine how the area must have looked all those years ago and how people survived in such an unforgiving environment. Surely it must have been cooler and wetter to support a population with time and energy to spend mixing and applying colors to rocks. Gannon requested that we not post photographs on social media out of respect for the sacred nature of the images for the Chumash people.

Evidence of the importance of this secluded area to other living creatures abounded. Patiently waiting for the intruders to leave, a pair of long-eared owls peered from the darkness of a cave high above us. A hawk circled watchfully in the patch of sky overhead. I stepped warily around piles of mouse-sized bones dropped by decades of raptors dining on the cliffs above.

Coyotes, foxes, badgers and other small mammals survived the farming era, but hunters long ago cleared the land of anything large and edible. In 1985, the area was one of the first in the state to reintroduce pronghorn and tule elk. Elk herds now exceed several hundred animals and are thriving. Pronghorns are not doing so well. Few fawns are fast enough to outrun coyotes, and although they are the fastest native North American animal, sometimes called the American antelope, adults cannot leap barbed wire fences to escape.

Simmler Road, a dirt track crossing to the east side of the Plain, is known as a popular spot for grazing elk. While resting in my vehicle for a refreshment break, I scoured the horizon for signs of life. Two distant brown shapes raised my hopes. But, detecting no movement after several minutes, I concluded they were just a couple of darker bushes.

Movement in my peripheral vision next caught my attention. Creeping up behind were two critters about the size of large goats. Through binoculars, brown topcoat, white belly and inward-curving antlers identified them as pronghorn. Over the next 15 minutes, I watched as they browsed, presumably aware of my vehicle but apparently unfazed. They approached within about 50 feet before strolling casually back into the brush. Although I never saw an elk, this unexpected encounter with the most threatened animal on the Plain gave credence to the Carrizo as "California's Serengeti."

I continued driving east along a dusty, unpaved road towards the Temblor Range and into the heart of a wildflower superbloom. Random purple spears of owl's clover penetrated a yellow ocean of goldfields. On higher ground, tidy tips' white-edged petals cast a lighter lemon hue. Towards mid-valley, the floral extravaganza faded into dense areas of immature Carrizo fiddleneck, their fuzzy leaves pregnant with buds ready to erupt into orange-tinged blooms. Occasional roadside clumps of frilly lemon's mustard glowed pink against this solid field of green.

The road rose steeply from the valley floor, twisting through loose rocks where eons of earth movement along the San Andreas Fault has ground the foothills into geological debris. In *Assembling California,* author John McPhee lists the showcase of landforms along this tectonic scar: "benches and scarps, its elongated grabens and beheaded channels, its desiccated sag ponds and dry deflected streams. From the air, the fault trace is keloid, virtually organic in its insistence and its creep—north forty degrees west."

Savoring a closer view of these features that had intrigued me over years of glimpses from the comfort of an airline seat on flights to Los Angeles, I headed north on Elkhorn Road. After miles of dodging deep ruts where others had become stuck in the mud, probably having ignored "Impassable When Wet" warnings to their peril, a sign announced my arrival at Wallace Creek.

I strode up a stony trail. At the top of the ridge, I stared into dramatic evidence of seismic forces that continue to shape California. About 3,800 years ago, Wallace Creek flowed downhill from the North American Plate straight across the restless San Andreas Fault to the open plain on the Pacific Plate. As that plate moved northwest, the creek bed bent into a channel that followed the fault line. On reaching its original course, the flow turned back out towards Soda Lake. Over time, that channel has grown to about 150 yards in length. Although the average is just over one inch per year, displacement here is not slow and steady. It happens in sudden jerks that we know as earthquakes. Geologists say that this section of the plain lurched 30 feet north in a few terrifying seconds during the devastating 7.9-magnitude Fort Tejon temblor of 1857.

I stared at the displaced creek bed carved into the peaceful hillside and pondered the tectonic energy silently building pressure in the earth beneath my feet. My curiosity overcome by a dose of caution, I decided it was time to set out for home. At any moment, the next Big One could unleash the raw power stored under this notorious seismic hotspot.

The last rays of sunlight shrank from the peaks of the Temblor Range as I headed north. Ahead, the brilliant glow from a meadow of yellow hillside daisies faded into memory as darkness filled the valley. My visit to the Carrizo Plain ended as it began with another reminder of Frost's ode to nature's ephemeral beauty: "Nothing gold can stay."

Camel shadows, Merzouga Dunes, Morocco

An Unexpected New Year's Eve in Luxor

Diane LeBow

On New Year's Eve in the working-class residential section of Luxor, Egypt, among muddy alleys and run-down tenements, I sat in the center of a small living room. Gathered around me were six young Egyptian men smoking hashish through a hookah. My fitted white St. Tropez skirt and flowing light-green silk blouse were so uncommon here that I felt almost like an untouchable. *Sort of like reverse nun wear*, I thought. My escort, a man I had met in my hotel lounge a few days before, was an archaeological guide, an occupation that seemed to be ubiquitous for young unmarried Egyptian men with some education. He and I spoke French, and he acted as translator.

The pouring rain had continued since I'd arrived here in Luxor a few days before from Cairo. I was traveling by public bus around Egypt, roundtrip through the Sinai to Sharm el Sheik for a dive trip and then back to Cairo, the hub for any public transportation. Small airports did not yet exist in many places in this country. Traveling by bus enabled me to see more of the country and meet everyday Egyptian people more easily, although few women rode on the buses at the time.

Checking into the Winter Palace in Luxor, Agatha Christie's home where she composed *Death on the Nile*, I unwound into the warmth and golden splendor. The hotel, built in 1886, exuded colonial extravagance with twinkling chandeliers, elaborate Egyptian-themed draperies and carpet, and attendants and waiters who pampered the fortunate clientele, including me.

Settling into my opulent room, I looked out at the Nile

flowing past and wondered if perhaps Agatha Christie had looked out this very window and was inspired by the view. I was very excited to be in the heart of ancient Thebes, Luxor's original name. Homer extols the city's opulence: "In Egyptian Thebes, the heaps of precious ingots gleam, the hundred-gated Thebes."

I dressed for the evening and went downstairs for cocktails and dinner. While I was relaxing in the lounge, a young man introduced himself as Ahmed, the aforementioned archeological guide. After we talked for a while, he asked if I had arranged my visit yet and offered to guide me around the Valley of the Kings and Queens during my stay. This sounded perfect, and I accepted.

Early the following morning, Ahmed picked me up at my hotel, and we traveled to the West Bank across the Nile for exploration of the famous tombs. I especially enjoyed trying to sink back into the consciousness of these tomb inhabitants by studying the images on the walls that depicted their selected necessities for the next life: foods, amphorae of drinks, animals (especially cats), carriages, slaves and servants, and of course gods. There they were as companions into eternity: the falcon-headed Horus, Hathor with her headdress of cow horns and a sun disk, Osiris the god of fertility and the dead, and their many colleagues. *Maybe it would be comforting to believe similarly in such a detailed next life*, I thought, but I really found it impossible to imagine. I have enough trouble packing for a few weeks' trip and couldn't imagine packing for eternity, although I suppose all those slaves and gods would be helpful in doing so.

At the end of our tour, Ahmed accompanied me back to

the Winter Palace where we had dinner. During the meal, I enjoyed watching my first authentic belly-dancing performance, realizing that classic belly dancers do, indeed, sport fleshy bellies. No anorexia in their ranks. During dinner, Ahmed said, "If you are free tomorrow evening, I would be honored if you would join me at my local friends' New Year's Eve party." He spoke French well, was witty, educated and well mannered, and this sounded like fun as well as an opportunity to experience more of the real Luxor. I gladly accepted.

The following evening around 9 p.m. we met in the hotel lobby. In front of the hotel, he flagged down a *calèche* or horse-drawn taxi, the main mode of transportation in Luxor at the time. Away from the tourist center and hotels, beggars and signs of poverty were all around us as we made our way into the working-class residential section. People and horses struggled for space along the muddy and eerily dark streets.

Our carriage came to a stop in front of a simple tan stucco apartment house, drying wash hanging out the windows and merchants with carts hawking goods in the street. Ahmed took my arm and we escaped the hubbub into the building and then walked up two flights of dimly lit stairs. The whole experience was both exciting and a bit overwhelming as I moved into a truly foreign world. Entering Ahmed's friends' flat, we met six young Egyptian men who were gathered around a hookah, smoking hashish. He introduced me as an American professor and writer from San Francisco and Paris. They took a break from their refreshment to stand and greet me politely if with some curiosity and awkwardness on both sides. The men were a few years younger than Ahmed, probably in their late thirties, dressed casually in jeans, cotton shirts and sweaters. One by one, each of the young men shook my hand in a formal manner. Teachers and professors are well respected in this culture. After a while, they invited me to share their hookah, which I did. It helped ease any cross-cultural tensions. Their sisters, wives or girlfriends peered in from the kitchen doorway and smiled timidly.

Tarek, the host, offered me a seat on an upholstered chair in the center of the small living room. Conversation moved slowly as all comments had to be translated by Ahmed into French for me, and my remarks had to be repeated in Arabic for the others. They asked about what life was like in the USA, about my students and about what I thought of Egypt. "I'm traveling alone in order to do research for my classes and my writing," I explained. This partly eased their curiosity about a single woman traveling by herself in their culture.

"This is a new experience for them," Ahmed explained. "They have never been in such an intimate setting with a non-Egyptian woman before."

Ditto for me, I thought.

While I chatted with the young men, their wives and female relatives remained clustered in the kitchen, cooking. Intermittently, they brought salads, meats and pastries into the room which they placed on the center table and then left without a word. I tried to make eye contact with them, asking Ahmed to translate for me. "What is your name?" "You are very pretty." "How do you make that dish?" Each answered shyly, lowering their dark lashes and turning away before returning to the kitchen where I could hear giggles and soft conversation.

After a couple of hours visiting, eating and sharing our

ideas for the new year, we all rose to leave. One of the young men I'd been chatting with invited me to see his new apartment before we departed. "I recently bought it and would be proud to show you. It took me a long time to save the money," he said.

"Of course," I replied without hesitation. "I'd be honored." Along with Ahmed, we walked to where his new apartment was up a dark, sticky flight of stairs. As we climbed, fatigue from the long day suddenly hit me, and I had second thoughts about what I was doing. Why was I going to look at the empty apartment of someone I had just met? But it was too late to backtrack so I followed them up the stairs. He unlocked the door and we entered a darkened, sparsely furnished flat. It smelled of dampness and wet plaster. In the gloom, I could make out one chair, a small table and a single unmade bed. The man in whose apartment we stood closed the door behind us and squared his shoulders as he said: "Aren't you worried about your safety coming into a place like this with two men?"

I had thought about this. Curiosity often draws me into these situations. How far can I push the experience? I really wasn't afraid. Actually, I had always been more leery of being trapped in the traditional woman's life of my era at home, dependent, with a husband and children, than I am when free to follow my curiosity on the road.

Relying on my hopefully untouchable reverse-nun magic mode, I took a deep breath and tried to exude calm. "Of course not," I replied. "With gentlemen like yourselves, I know that I am well protected." The unstated but palpable tension in the room deflated and we all smiled and made light conversation. Ahmed and I said our farewells, exited and took a *calèche* back to the Winter Palace where Ahmed and I said our goodbyes. Walking up the marble hotel stairs and through doors opened by liveried doormen, I returned from one Egyptian world and entered another. Although this was not at all the same as the extreme travel depicted in the tombs—from life to the afterworld—I was still experiencing how different worlds can exist within one culture.

In the morning, on the bus heading to Aswan, my next stop, my heart raced a little when I thought about the possibly risky situation I had been in. Without realizing it, I had appealed to the less recognized side of machismo that involves honor, respect and nurturance—and it worked.

These young men sought my respect and understanding as much as I did theirs. For me, one of the joys of travel is sharing our common humanity, no matter our lack of a common language or culture. This remains a special New Year's Eve memory for me.

Old Meets New: Stunning architecture, gorgeous garments and ubiquitous iPhones in modern Shanghai

Three Girl Guides, China Style

Effin Older

It was my first trip to China, a 12-day guided tour that included Beijing, Shanghai, The Great Wall, Terracotta Warriors and to my surprise, eye-opening stories from the lives of our three Chinese guides—Abby, Stephanie and Cindy.

Besides being experts in China, past and present, they regaled us with personal details that I'll remember long after I've forgotten which emperor ruled which dynasty and how many hundreds of concubines he had.

Here are the girl-guide stories, beginning with Abby:

"You can ask anything, and photograph anyone and anything," she says. That's a relief. I was worried I'd innocently take a forbidden photo and end up who knows where. She quickly adds that we should get used to being pushed. "It's not that people are rude; it's that there are so many people. And, oh yes, there are no driving rules, so be careful."

No kidding. Intersections were a terrifying tangle of cars, bicycles, scooters and buses, all racing in random directions and no one slowing down. Definitely life-threatening. There are 8 million cars in Beijing, and Abby doesn't own one of them. So, she takes the BMW—*bus, metro, walk.* Sounds much safer to me.

"I'm sure you're all curious about the emperor's concubines," Abby says. "Here are the qualifications: She must be a virgin between 13 and 17; no stinky breath or underarms; strong body [girls were stripped naked to inspect their shoulders, arms, backs and legs]; and skilled in chess and massage, painting and calligraphy. Some emperors had thousands of concubines, and that's *before* Viagra. Any volunteers?"

Abby grew up poor. Her family used a shared bathroom in the community courtyard; she knew all her neighbors. Today, she lives in a condo, and after 15 years, she's never spoken to any of her neighbors. "Changing times," she says ruefully.

Abby paid a million yuan (US$143,000) for her condo; it's now worth four. She lives there with her husband, son and parents. The one-child policy is no more, but even so, Abby wouldn't have two children. "If I had another son, I'd be broke. Parents have to buy a condo for their sons when they marry. I can't afford two!"

I perk up when Abby tells us the secret to not getting gray hair: "Eat black sesame seeds!" Later that day, as we watch elderly folks exercise in a park, she says, "The men all dye their hair." (But what about black sesame seeds? I don't point out the contradiction.)

In Tiananmen Square, under a giant picture of Mao, Abby acknowledges that, yes, 3,000 students were massacred 30 years ago. "It was for the good of China. It wasn't possible to have two competing governments," she says without batting an eye.

I'm in China. I don't bat an eye either. I also keep my mouth shut when she describes the birth of her son. "After the birth, I didn't wash my body, my hair, or brush my teeth for 30 days. I used a dry cloth to wipe my hands and feet." Why? "To prevent arthritis." She does a little dance. "See? It worked."

I ask our second guide, Cindy, about not washing after giving birth. "What?! I took a shower immediately." She adds, "And I don't have arthritis."

Cindy was born during the Cultural Revolution and went to the Tiananmen Square demonstration as a student. That meant no foreign travel for her for several years. "Then, as an unmarried woman, I was 'too dangerous,'" she explains. "Mao brainwashed us." Once married, she got the okay to travel; now Cindy regularly leads groups of Chinese tourists through Europe and North America.

She loves her job, but as an "office girl," she'll have to retire at 55; female laborers retire at 50, men at 65. No choice. "Even so, women have climbed from lowest class to second class. And at home, women are in charge. We say, "Happy wife; happy life." Our husbands agree."

Cindy's parents had a matchmaker; they never touched before marriage. Her grandmother had bound feet and raised seven children. "Times have changed," says Cindy, echoing Abby. Her mother gave her this advice when she was young: Before marriage, open your eyes as big as you can; once married, close one eye. Once you have a baby, close both eyes.

Cindy has one daughter. "My mom took over raising her at four months so I could travel for my job. She wants me to keep pace with the times. She says I must eat quality food, not junk food like young people today. I don't want their nine-nine-six lifestyle—work 9 a.m. to 9 p.m., six days a week. Not good."

To relieve stress, Cindy goes to a Buddhist temple to breathe deeply, concentrate and relax. Probably a good idea since she calls herself a road killer. "I drive a Peugeot. It's a strong car, not like Toyotas; they're soft. I need a strong car to survive an accident." After dodging traffic in China, I'm all about Peugeots.

Like Abby and Cindy, our third guide, Stephanie, has just one child, a son. Does she want another? "No! Too much homework!" Every night, she helps her son with his homework, which they usually finish around 11 p.m. That's after he's been in school from 7 a.m. to 6 p.m.

"I have to sign my name on the homework. If there's a mistake, I'm ridiculed by the teacher and other parents. My husband never helps. I'm Buddha mom; he's Disney dad—no punishment, just fun." Pause. "My son doesn't like me." Longer pause. "I don't like him either. He's 12, and his grandmother still feeds him with a spoon. He's like a little emperor."

Twelve days gave me a tiny glimpse into modern China, a country forging ahead while still holding a tight rein on its 1.4 billion people. Our three girl guides were all savvy world travelers, and yet, deep-rooted traditions still guide their lives. To guarantee his future success, Stephanie had a fortune teller name her son. Cindy let her mother bring up her four-month-old daughter. Abby eats black sesame seeds to avoid gray hair.

Stephanie and Abby both have young sons. Will they be desirable bachelors when the time comes? Stephanie defines desirable: They must have all five Cs—car, cash, credit card, condo and career.

I suspect their mothers will ensure they have all five. Especially Stephanie's little emperor.

A Northern Elephant Seal protects her pup at Piedras Blancas
Rookery after a disastrous morning

They Never Saw the Rainbow

Donna Peck

If all went well, I would hold my granddaughter in four weeks. My daughter, my only child, was resting and well taken care of. But I felt restless, like a raincloud about to burst. Since I wasn't needed, I packed up the car and sped south from San Francisco, leaving the main highway at Paso Robles, arriving at the coast with a flutter of excitement. In winter 5,000 pups are born at the elephant seal colony north of San Simeon.

The night manager at Morgan Hotel tapped a spot on the map as he slid it across: "Mudslide 15 miles north at Ragged Point." Seasonal shutdowns of Highway One put everyone at the mercy of the elements, including visitors.

The daytime desk clerk apologized; yes, cold showers could be quite miserable. The plumber had been summoned to replace the hot water heater, but he was swamped with calls. She offered a voucher for a nearby hotel. No time. I didn't want to miss the main event: Females give birth an hour after sunrise.

Rain splattered my face as I opened the car door at Piedras Blancas Elephant Seal Rookery. I sloshed through the flooded parking lot in rubber boots, then raced along the boardwalk under my umbrella, camera bag swinging, toward a swarm of seagulls and—good god!—froze on the spot. My city-bred brain couldn't make sense of the mayhem.

Crashing onto the narrow birthing beach, a record high tide plus 15-foot waves from an offshore swell created havoc.

An elephant seal bull bellowed at the advancing waves. He was the male alpha—a monster at the far fringe of imaginability, a horrific thing, 5,000 pounds of bone-crushing blubber, its broad chest scarred and slashed, its nose the ugliest appendage in creation: wobbling, fleshy, inflatable. The air blasting through his nose didn't match the storm's sound and fury.

No mistaking the females: They were having a disastrous morning. The high tide had pushed the seals against the boardwalk. Squeezed onto a narrow stretch, they were going nuts, flipping sand over their bodies in furious arcs. Up and down the beach, sand was flying.

No mistaking where births were happening: Seagulls flapped and squawked overhead. A pup slid out, and the gulls dove into the churning red water. I felt sick. They chased the receding tide, pecking at clumps of afterbirth.

The gulls abandoned their bloody meal as a wall of water slammed the beach and swamped the birthing/nursing areas. Masses of bodies writhed and blew apart: pups torn from the nipple, mothers howling in alarm. A giant female torpedoed over mounds of rolling rippling flesh chasing the receding tide. Wet cocoon-shaped bodies floated away in the surge. "Gone, my baby's gone." Everywhere tortured cries. My maternal instinct screamed at me to help. The half-dozen faces around me on the viewing platform registered the same breathless worry.

The big swells withdrew, leaving a dry patch of sand about 15 feet wide the length of the beach. The alpha swayed on his front flippers. A pup had floated to the water's edge where it lay motionless, its body covered in glossy black fur.

Dave, the 80-year-old docent from Piedras Blancas Friends of the Elephant Seal, stroked his whiskers. "The newborn pups are not very mobile," he told us. "They don't know how to swim, so high tides and high surf cause trouble."

Dave's even delivery was at odds with my racing heart. Dozens of newborn pups had been separated from their mothers. Thousands of newborns die in winter storms. Anguish welled up inside me. I thought of my pregnant daughter giving birth in four weeks. What if something went wrong? She's at risk. Her baby's at risk. I remembered giving birth and asking for drugs. Then the midwife's calm, encouraging words mounted to growing excitement. "I see the head." She repositioned me on the bed and I let it all go: my voice, my fatigue and bore down. Pressure eased. I felt relief but also a shudder of fear. The next moment changed everything. I reached down and pulled my baby onto my chest. Gray slime covered her skin, I touched her all over and patted her fuzzy wet head. What a beauty. Her first sound, too melodious to be a cry, seared my heart. Her eyes looked for me. Love, an eternity of love, flowed between us.

"Can't see a thing in this swell," Dave's voice wavered. His gnarled knuckles gripped the binoculars. Great white sharks were out there patrolling, but he didn't want to say. I felt helpless. I hated the ocean for taking the lives of the newborns, their first breath their last.

Dave led us to another observation deck to where roughly 200 females sprawled on the wet sand. After the water drained, the howling subsided as the newborns suckled again. Some mothers had no suckling pup, others had two suckling: hers plus an orphan. "Both pups will die," Dave said. I flinched. A mother nursing two pups meant that neither one would survive. A pup needed a full supply of milk to develop enough body weight to out-swim sharks.

Umbrellas snapped shut. An elated buzz traveled along the boardwalk. Above Dave's head, a rainbow blossomed in the sky, like a bouquet of flowers at a gravesite.

"Woohwoohwoooh," Dave whistled long and low as the rainbow pushed out a full arc of color across the northwest sky from land to ocean. I stayed behind after the red, orange, yellow, green. blue, lavender drained from the sky, watching for those who never saw the rainbow.

The night brought grumbling hotel guests to the lobby. But it wasn't a hot shower that I missed. I needed to see my daughter.

Driving back to San Francisco, the afternoon sun gave way to dark skies and a steady downpour. Life throws me back and forth between beauty and terror: the beauty of life and the fear of losing the ones most dear to me.

A month later, when my granddaughter was placed in my arms, eternity peered out from her round dark eyes. She smelled of breast milk and the ocean.

Since that morning at the Piedras Blancas, the precarious existence of creatures and humans has escalated. The world's at risk. The large-scale loss of life was unthinkable a few weeks before the 2020 pandemic. The beauty of spring mocked the daily reports of global sorrow. Yet six feet apart, people walked their neighborhoods, admiring the pink jasmine and calla lilies, enjoying the clean air, while a virus, to quote Rilke, "serenely disdains to destroy us."

Penny Falls, above Clayoquot Sound, on Vancouver Island, British Columbia, a short, rather steep hike up from the Clayoquot Wilderness Lodge

Lost Horizon

Alec Scott

Hello, Vertigo, my old friend. I grin nervously at my fellow passengers as the floatplane hefts itself out of the muddy Fraser River and heads toward the snow-capped mountains of Vancouver Island. The pilot gets the 10 seater aloft, banking up by a skating arena built for the 2010 Olympic Games and then over a series of suburban homes set in tidy, fenced-in tracts. No doubt each of the plane's nine passengers has a mix of reasons for leaving all of this behind—the competition and conformity of modern urban life—and heading for an isolated lodge on an estuary in Clayoquot Sound.

My mix feels a bit of a muddle, something I want to sort out in the wilds, away from my always-demanding devices. But first there's the vertigo to weather—the mild nausea, the feeling of spinning and overall unsteadiness. Oy. Eyes forward, I search my brain for some half-remembered trivia, a rosary to dispel my fear of flying in a small plane; Vancouver was named after English naval officer George Vancouver, right? Or was it John? Ringo, maybe? Google won't be at my fingertips where we're going.

Clayoquot—pronounced "clack-watt"—covers 1,000 square miles of land and water, an area half the size of Wales. A part of Canada's only temperate rainforest blankets its islands and the lowlands that border the saltwater inlets and fresh-water rivers. A range of tall mountains, much older than the mainland's Rockies, protects the UNESCO world biosphere reserve, located halfway up the rugged Pacific Coast of Vancouver Island.

Our plane weaves through the peaks, so near-seeming now that they call to mind, to this mind anyway, the mid-Himalayas plane crash that begins *Lost Horizon*. But our landing is gentle. The plane just slips into a fjord turned golden by the afternoon sun. Cupped by mountains, an estuary is dotted with big one-story log buildings and white safari tents on large platforms. My phone has zero bars on it—and I'm thrilled.

The Danish Prince Joachim and his French bride, Princess Marie, spent their honeymoon in seclusion here at the Clayoquot Wilderness Resort—as European tabloid reporters tried, unsuccessfully, to track them down. I'm also here celebrating recent nuptials, though no paparazzi are after my fellow, now husband, and me. And I'm turning 50 in two days, so there's that. Most importantly, we're marking the end of a rough couple of years.

In June 2015, David came home to tell me, in his careful, undramatic way, that apparently there was an unusual growth in his brain. Three months later, a top surgeon removed the tangerine-sized tumor. To prevent its regrowth, David has since endured a long course of chemo, working all the while at a demanding job. Such things as these focus the mind, and after 11 years together, we decided to make our bond official, to do a small, slender gay wedding at San Francisco's City Hall. All of this feels—and is—more important than my hurtling too fast toward 50, but there's still a part of me wanting to tote up the wins and losses to date. This is the muddle I've come here to process.

A wagon pulled by a team of caramel-colored Norwegian draft horses brings us from the dock to the main lodge (constructed of logs recovered from the river bottom), where flutes of champagne and sushi rolls await by antique armchairs and lit fireplaces.

This luxe lodge, the unlikely dream of a Canadian financier, Rick Genovese, aspires to be among the world's most ecologically friendly. The son of working-class Italian immigrants from outside Toronto, Genovese came to the Sound to fish and liked the place so much he bought this site, an old gold-mining camp. "We cleaned it up some, and now we have that doctor's goal in mind," he says. "First, do no harm."

And so, he added closed waste and composting systems to keep the resort's pollutants from escaping. After hearing that fish counts in the nearby Bedwell River were low, he invested $3 million to restore salmon spawning grounds—and the fish counts are now up.

"Basically, I want our guests to fall for this area like I did." And so, in front of an outdoor hearth, the young, eco-minded staff begin signing us up for excursions to see this mostly untouched wilderness up close. A Zodiac trip to see marine wildlife. A surf lesson on an isolated beach.

As we sip champagne, it all feels ultra-civilized, but we're reminded of where we are when we're asked to empty our suitcases of any food since bears will not hesitate to claw their way into our riverside safari tents in search of the same. One of our fellow floatplane passengers, a tall, gregarious blonde from Louisiana, empties enough food from her luggage to nourish herself, easily, for a month.

We're to stay, for the next few days, in an absurdly well-appointed tent worthy of *Out of Africa*, one with an Oriental rug, carriage bed and antique dresser. (Tents, we're told, because they are more easily removed each winter.) Ours over-looks the place where the river and the sea greet each other, the salty tides that come in and out keeping mosquito counts blessedly low. I wash up, pre-dinner, in an outdoor shower, looking up into some tall conifers, breathing in that loamy smell of decomposing needles. Some of the forest's noises are familiar: crows cawing, woodpeckers rat-tat-tatting away. Others are not. Was that weird keening followed by a coo an owl? Spooky.

We wander over the grounds, coming across a big ship-ping container that has been perched next to the estuary, given a glass side and converted into a nautical-themed room with a lifejacket from the Queen Mary hung on a wall. At the center is a billiard table with its balls arranged in the custom-ary triangle. "Surreal," David says, and I break. For spectators, we have a pair of black-and-white mergansers who sit across a channel from us on a gravel bed exposed by the low tide.

In the late morning the next day, I find myself belaying up a conifer when halfway up, my arms and nerve both give out. David calls up to me offering encouragement from below. The truth is that for a while, I've been the cheerleader in our twosome. It feels great to have him egging me on, and I nearly get there. (I'm not too proud to admit a guide hoists me the last 10 feet.) The reward: some friendly, chipmunk-sized squirrels visit, evidently not yet jaded by frequent contact with humans.

On the day of my birthday, a mountainside hike near the lodge brings about a different kind of challenge. Brain surgery often compromises one's sense of balance, but David adeptly makes his way through this hike's challenges over a shale field with rocks that give way underfoot, up bits so steep that we need to pull ourselves up by the trailside ropes. At hike's end, we happily stand by the cold spray in front of 50-foot-tall Penny Falls.

"We made it," I say, referring both to the hike and the mainly upward slog from David's operation.

That evening over delicate, citrusy crab ravioli with foraged wild chives and lamb that's been slow-cooked in black garlic and balsamic, we recount the day's adventures: the hike and a surfing lesson. At the meal's close, the Swiss pastry chef serves up a candlelit chocolate cake on a flat rock used as a plate while the kitchen team and other guests sing "Happy Birthday." I often feel awkward when the limelight falls on me, but this evening I think, simply, "Bring it," as I blow out the candles and let the bittersweet chocolaty cake melt on my tongue.

Late that night, the stars wheel above the deck in front of our tent. They come in various colors here, far from any big city's bright lights, and around the Big Dipper and the belted Orion are thousands upon thousands more, less familiar ones. We sit in companionable silence, both of us, I suspect, feeling that peculiarly comforting sensation of minuteness.

There's a brisk headwind coming at us from the ocean, and the swells are such that they lift our inflatable Zodiac motorboat at a 45-degree angle then slam us down. Sheets of cold saltwater soon drench us. Even our seasoned pilot, a built, bearded former barge captain, is concerned.

A nearby sea otter seems less anxious as he lies on his back among bull-kelp heads, using a rock to open a mussel. Otters here were hunted almost to extinction, but their numbers are recovering thanks to conservation efforts and hunting restrictions. So says our guide, a young woman whose resort name is Baby Giraffe—this because she's tall and adorably awkward. She tells us the otters spend 90 percent of their lives lying on their backs, floating on this huge waterbed. "Must be nice," says David, diligent to a fault.

The wind and swells pick up even more, and after some particularly violent slams, our captain decides we're done seeking out orcas, taking the boat into a sheltered cove. I'm disappointed, but where we head instead is a place I've been hearing about since I was a kid growing up in Ontario: the Big Tree Trail on Meares Island.

In the 1980s and '90s, a ragtag group of environmentalists and local native leaders fought to preserve the old-growth forest on Meares Island, among others. The long-simmering struggle—the so-called War of the Woods—came to a boil in 1993 with what has been called the largest act of civil disobedience in Canadian history (police arrested more than 800 of those blocking the loggers). Baby Giraffe, who grew up around here, remembers that they used her school as a jail after the regular one filled up. But, in the end, the protest worked, and this forest, among others, has been saved.

Today, it's still home to hundreds of giant red cedar, among them a tree known as the Hanging Garden, a 1,500-plus-year-old colossus with hundreds of ferns and other plants growing on it. No wonder this coast's indigenous people call the cedar the "tree of life"—traditionally, they made many uses of the trees, stripping sections of bark to make rope and clothing, taking chunks out of the trees as building materials. "The trees can generally survive these things," Baby Giraffe says. I think of one of David's doctors talking about how his brain would rewire after the operation to compensate for the lost bits of his frontal lobe.

Two years ago, after the removal of the tumor, in his hospital bed in Redwood City, they asked him a standard test question: Where are you? His reply was St. Pancras; the train station was a place we'd driven past once in a taxi on a trip to London. That was a species of vertigo, too: I worried I'd lost him then.

On the boat ride back, we spot a brown bear with her two cubs on a beach at low tide, the mother turning over stones to feast on barnacles under them. Their eyesight is as poor as their sense of smell is keen, and as the wind is coming off the land, we're able to bring the boat in close. The cubs are playful, cat-sized, their brown-black fur more lustrous than their mom's. She lifts her snout and sends her cubs back into the safety of the forest. She continues eating for a bit before following her little ones into the bush.

"You can read the land's history—where the landslides were, where long gone native villages were—because that's where the red alders are," says our guide Jamie during a kayak outing. Bearded, with a gymnast's body, he's an amateur botanist and historian who's nearly completed his design degree at Vancouver's top art college. "People are proud of Canada with lots of justification. But in this area, there hasn't been all that much to be proud of."

He's speaking about the treatment of the people who have long occupied this coast, the Nuu-Chah-Nulth, a group famous for its dugout canoes and totem poles. Jamie describes the pre-contact life in such villages, the foods they foraged from these woods, the days-long ceremonies called potlatches in which hosts gave away many of their possessions to guests. The Canadian government banned potlatch festivals for years, he says, and removed children from their families, placing them in Christian religious boarding schools.

The next day, I hear more about how this land's first occupants have fared. The resort often arranges helicopter tours of the area, and a hereditary chief of the Ahousat, one of the tribes of the Nuu-Chah-Nulth nation, joins us on ours. Wearing a T-shirt with a raven totem on it, Maquinna Lewis George is a soft-spoken, dignified man of medium stature. I get into the chopper's front seat, noting with dread the glass bottom below me. I extend my hand to George, seated in the back.

The helicopter goes up over a rise and (gulp) plunges down the other side. "My great-great-grandfather climbed that mountain before making war on another tribe, one that would not share the resources," he says as a bald eagle flies nearby. "He cleansed himself in a lake halfway up. You have a place to do that, where you get your power, but you don't tell others where it is. He prayed on the mountaintop. We won the war and took over their lands—and we took their war song."

The helicopter lands on a gravel creekbed, and holding hands to keep from falling, the Chief and I wade across a swift-flowing channel to the shore. Our bare feet sinking into the luxuriant moss, enter another old-growth forest and pass a bear den in the hollowed-out base of a red cedar as he speaks of his own, brutal experience in a residential school. "They wanted to educate the Indian out of you. Or, if not, to beat it out of you."

The tall cedars let sun shafts penetrate the canopy all about us, lending a cathedral feel to this space. George's grandson, an aspiring photographer, takes shots of the sun-pierced woods while George sings the war song, undeterred by the mosquitoes buzzing about him. It's in a minor chord with about five notes, the lyrics full of long ahs and ohs that are gentle but determined.

I ask him about the Nuu-Chah-Nulth's recent legal victory in its long fight to manage the commercial fishery in Clayoquot ("We won round one, but the decision is under appeal") and about the native-owned forestry companies that are taking the lead in a new mode of logging here, one that identifies particular trees to cull, rather than clear-cutting ("Jobs—in fishing and lumber—they're as important to us as to anyone else").

As a result of the press coverage of the War in the Woods and the UNESCO designation, tourism is up, and George tells me members of his tribe are also increasingly finding jobs in the growing ecotourism sector, leading whale-watching tours and guiding hikes through tribal lands. "We're on the road back," says George. "I mean, we never went away, but our rights, they're beginning to be recognized."

On the floatplane ride back to the City of Vancouver, winds off the Pacific buffet the plane, and the vertigo comes back. In a few minutes, we'll land in the still muddy Fraser and my cell phone will light up with a slew of urgent emails and texts.

A sight out the plane's window helps to distract me from my stomach's relentless churn while also clarifying what I made of the mental muddle that came along with me on this journey.

Below us, I see a copse of what I now know to be red alders running down a mountainside. Jamie's lesson: The trees have probably grown on the site of a former landslide. Snatches of the lyrics from an old, much-covered Fleetwood Mac song present themselves: "The landslide brought me down...Well, I've been afraid of changing, 'cause I've built my life around you."

The song talks of the growth that can happen after a big crisis, a landslide. I stretch the metaphor a bit, maybe past the breaking point.

Here in Clayoquot, the otters are back from near-extinction caused by the landslide of overhunting. With Genovese's help, the salmon are returning in greater numbers to the Bedwell, a river threatened by runoff from the old mines and the camp that used to sit where the resort now does. Chief George's people are doing their best to recover from and to persist through the ongoing landslide that began for them when the first Europeans, George Vancouver among them, sailed into Clayoquot Sound, bearing their dread guns and diseases.

On the more personal side, two years ago, a landslide hit David—and me. We weren't buried by it, though it felt like a near thing sometimes. I wouldn't have imagined at the time that, under a waterfall's spray, we'd be able to manage a triple celebration of my 50th, of our marriage, of his strong comeback. When we sit under the stars, we know how small, how temporary all our victories are, but that doesn't make them any less sweet.

In the jump seat ahead of me, David's oblivious to my vertigo, unburdened by my rather earnest internal monologue. Instead, he's chatting away with the pilot, evidently enjoying the hell out of the ride.

Earl Terwilliger beside the door of a military tent
during World War II

In My Father's Footsteps:
A Marine's Daughter Tracks Down Dad's
World War II Hawaii

Carole Terwilliger Meyers

On the 50th anniversary of the attack on Pearl Harbor, President George H.W. Bush declared, "The war is over. It is history." But the war is not over. And it never will be over for those who fought in it, or for their children who lived with the aftermath of human anguish.

As my cruise ship sails out of the harbor, the soft, warm tropical air caresses my skin. I look out over the twinkling lights of Waikiki—just as my dad did when he sailed off to surprise the Japanese in battle in the Marshall Islands on January 15, 1944. Except that my father's troopship, holding about 2,000 men, was completely dark, and the sailors weren't permitted even to whisper. Their exit had to be silent due to the secrecy of their mission.

Just a bunch of excited American kids waiting to test their teenage muscles, they believed they were sailing off to fight gloriously in retaliation for the December 7, 1941, attack on Pearl Harbor, in which more than 2,300 American military personnel were killed—1,177 of whom were sailors and Marines aboard the USS *Arizona*. But in reality, they were sailing straight into hell, and they were still too young and too innocent to be suitably afraid. That night, my dad found himself floating past the sunken *Arizona*—a ship he had sailed on five times during his first enlistment. He has never put in words what that felt like.

My dad, Earl Walter Terwilliger, a three-stripe sergeant, was only 22 years old. He says that while he and his fellow Marines were waiting there in Honolulu Harbor to sail out to the unknown of battle in the Pacific (which turned out to be on Engebi Island in the Eniwetok Atoll, where he remembers landing under fire and proudly recalls his unit setting a world record for taking an island—eight hours and two minutes), he could hear the sounds of people partying on shore. It is fitting that the music I hear played by my cruise ship's sendoff band more than 50 years later is from that era and includes the nostalgic, upbeat "In the Mood."

The ship I am sailing on is a testament to what humankind can accomplish in peacetime and also a testament to what my father and his buddies went to war for—to assure that a party ship full of happy people can sail out of this harbor for a peaceful pleasure cruise.

While I enjoy accommodations in a spacious stateroom with a porthole, my dad's lot was sleeping crammed into a bunk, or hanging from a hammock, or stuffed into a bedding roll on a crowded deck. While I dine on fresh fruit and the bounty of the Islands in a full-service dining room, he was chowing down on rations or eating in the mess hall (though he complains about none of this and remembers being wellfed). He sailed anticipating adventure but instead found horror; I sail anticipating relaxation but discover enlightenment.

I am taking this most American of cruises primarily for pleasure but also with the intent of using shore excursions to check out some of the military sites in Hawaii my dad has spoken of. I want to follow his footsteps to try to catch a glimpse of his stride through time just like when, as a child, I trailed behind while trying to keep up with his fast-paced feet, usually shod in combat boots.

It wasn't until my dad was in his seventies that I got the real story of his military service. As a child, stories of "The War" held little interest for me. Periodically, he would ceremoniously open his footlocker and take out his battlefield souvenirs, among them his dog tags, the ripped helmet chinstrap that deflected shrapnel from his head and probably saved his life and a torn white Japanese flag with a big red dot in the center. My siblings and I would look at these objects with a limited understanding of their history and importance, and unfortunately, he would tell us very little about how he acquired them. Then he carefully packed everything back into a past he kept stuffed securely in his trunk.

The full tragedy of his war experience didn't come back to haunt him until he retired and finally had time to reflect. Then, when I was an adult with grown children of my own, just prior to my leaving on a vacation to Hawaii, Dad mentioned that he had been stationed on Maui. He told me he trained there with the 22nd Marines (he later joined the 5th Amphibious Corps and previously fought with the 3rd Marine Raiders in the Wallis Islands), doing drills on the snow-covered Haleakala volcano to "thicken our blood" for the coming Pacific battles. Something finally clicked. I was intrigued. I wanted to know more.

Our first port is Nawiliwili Harbor, near Lihue on Kauai, where on a shore excursion I face some of my own demons by remaining in a kayak that I am sure will dump me in the drink. Instead of drowning, I get the hang of it and enjoy a peaceful float down the Huleia River, the very river that Indiana Jones swung over on a rope while making his daring movie escape. In a fabulous ending to the excursion, we trample barefoot over a muddy path through a dense, jungle-like expanse, bringing to mind my dad's tale of contracting filariasis (an illness brought on by a particular kind of mosquito that deposits eggs in the bloodstream which then hatch into worms) in the violent circumstances of his very different jungle visit in the Wallis and Marshall Islands. The parasitic worms blocked off the blood vessels in his arm, which swelled to three times its normal size as he developed elephantiasis. (But Dad credits the mosquitoes that bit him, and luck, with saving his life. Because of his disability, he was sent back home through New Caledonia and wound up missing some of the war's even nastier, more bitter battles. And he also credits that training stint in Maui with actually thickening his blood and thus keeping him from bleeding to death from the wounds that earned him a Purple Heart.)

Our next port is Wailuku on Maui, where my dad's unit R&R'd. Here my husband and I rent a car so we can go wherever our leads direct us. Wailuku is such a sleepy town that it requires a real stretch to imagine it jumping with Marines on their night off. It is so un-touristy that I'm unable to find a promotional T-shirt or a baseball cap to send back to my dad. But while I'm searching for such a souvenir, I start chatting in the town music shop with a good-natured, spacey fellow who seems interested in my mission. He tells me that the World War II "jarheads," as he calls them (a slang term referring to their general stubbornness), trained out at Haiku. He thinks the training grounds are a park now.

Dad never mentioned Haiku, and doesn't remember it when I describe it to him later, but we find the town on the map and set out. In hip Paia, we pick up a picnic lunch and drive on to Honomanu Bay. Here we are entertained by colorful windsurfers dancing on the turquoise surf while we eat, stretched out in the warm sand. I realize later that this fabulously beautiful spot must have been what my dad and his buddies saw, minus the windsurfers, as their buses and trucks rumbled down the zigzagging, then-unpaved mountain road into town.

When I ask the clerk in Haiku's little town store where the Marine base was in World War II, she hasn't a clue. The only other person in the store pipes up that there is a memorial park just outside of town. A few minutes later, we arrive at a large open field edged surprisingly with mature eucalyptus trees—I was expecting coconut palms—and with a sign declaring it the Fourth Marine Division Memorial Park. As we walk over the expanse of grass, I picture the field filled with tents and 5,000 excited young men, all of whom were volunteers. (My dad says the Marine Corps is "a year older than the United States." It began as a group of sailors who knew how to fire guns and is the only branch of the armed services made up entirely of enlisted men who volunteer their lives for defense.)

Dad says they were told never to eat any fruit found on the ground because it might be contaminated. So, while training in paradise, these young men devised a way to let off steam, practice their battle skills and get a snack all at the same time: One soldier would shoot down a coconut, aiming at the stem, while another caught it. Then they used their combat knives to cut the nuts open. (This was the same knife my daddy would later grab from his bedstead when I came to his room as a child, afraid of suspicious night noises outside my bedroom window. He then stomped right out into the night, as if on a skirmish, in search of the enemy. Once a Marine, always a Marine. However, he says he gave up his guns—among them two Colt .45 automatics that he once holstered cowboy-style onto each hip—when he left the service. He says he fired his last shot at the enemy and has never again discharged a gun.) These soldiers also practiced playing dead as hairy black banana spiders crawled over their bodies.

It was probably also here that this young man, my father, transformed his childhood talent for pitching baseballs into a life-saving skill at lobbing grenades. Later, in combat, instead of throwing balls to help his team win a game, he would be tossing grenades to keep his buddies alive.

After the war, the people of Maui erected a simple memorial in the park. I cry as I read:

THIS PLAQUE MARKS THE SITE OF CAMP
MAUI WORLD WAR II—HOME OF THE 4TH
MARINE DIVISION AFFECTIONATELY AND
PROUDLY CALLED "MAUI'S OWN."

This gratitude surprises me. I have to tweak my memory to recall that at the time of World War II, Hawaii was not a state. I had assumed the local residents might be annoyed by the Marines invading their town and island. Instead, the people of Maui very much appreciated what these young men were sacrificing for them.

Unlike so many other men in that brutal war, my dad came back alive. But like most men who survived, he was scarred, both on the outside and the inside. On the outside, he suffered a head injury from shrapnel that scarred his scalp and brain, causing him to have occasional epileptic seizures. (I've seen him suffer a seizure only once. It occurred recently while he was telling me the devastatingly emotional story of his innocence lost as a Marine in battle, "earning" his Purple Heart. He broke down as he told me about Corporal Snyder, who came to check on my dad's injuries after he was hit in the head by shrapnel. Part of the corporal's face was blown away as my father watched, horrified. Dad never saw him again, and he doesn't know if he survived.)

On the inside, he is an open wound. Like the Vietnam vets, he still has flashbacks and bad dreams. And like the Vietnam vets, he came home to a world where no one really wanted to hear the true story of what he had been through. So, like any Marine worth his salt, he kept all the horror, all the blood and guts, inside, where he thought they belonged. A few years ago when he joined a Vietnam vets therapy group, I found it surprising that these younger men welcomed him; they had no problem accepting him. But I shouldn't have been surprised because they all had fought, and are still fighting, the same battle. War, it turns out, is war. (In light of this, what a shame it is that the Veteran's Administration stopped hosting his group, and others like it, due to lack of funding. It is my opinion that all men who experience battle should be decompressed with group or individual counseling that addresses their trauma and that it should be paid for by "we the people.")

After strolling through the memorial park, watching happy children frolicking on the contemporary playground, we continue driving on up the mountain. I try to imagine what my father had been feeling when he went upcountry on "blood-thickening" excursions to the snow. We are running late and have to get back to the ship, so we turn our car around before reaching the top, where, even with no snow, it is still quite chilly.

Our ship makes several more stops. On the Big Island, we drop the search for the past and vacation for a while, walking lush paths through exotic landscaping at the spectacular Hawaii Tropical Botanical Garden in Hilo and diving in the Atlantis submarine off Kona. I have enough of this submarine in 45 minutes to last a lifetime and cannot help drifting into a daydream about the men who, more than 50 years ago, served their country squashed into such tight quarters during seemingly endless tours of duty. I find out later from my dad that he and his fellow Marine Raiders were often picked up after a battle in the South Pacific night by submarines. He says they would escape by sliding down the torpedo tube, which was only about a foot and a half in diameter, landing on mattresses.

Back in Honolulu, at the end of our voyage, we join a post-cruise shore excursion to the USS *Arizona* Memorial in Pearl Harbor. This is Hawaii's second most popular visitor attraction. (Number one is the National Memorial Cemetery of the Pacific at Punchbowl.) On the bus ride there, the mood is somber and the driver cracks not a joke. We learn that one of our tour members is a rare survivor of the Japanese attack.

Emotions start heating up in the *Arizona* museum, where I view letters home from very young men, many just teenagers, and see images of baby-faced soldiers that look like my dad in his enlistment photo—and like my son in his high school graduation picture.

After a silent boat ride out to the memorial, which floats above the famous sunken ship without touching it, I place my fragrant orange flower lei among the many purple orchid and white plumeria leis already piled at the base of the marble wall engraved tightly with the names of all the men who died here. Though traditionally leis are left for the crew that went down on the *Arizona*, I leave mine in memory of all servicemen. As tinkling bells play "Amazing Grace" and then the "Marine's Hymn," I, and many others, weep. A very light rain seems to be saying that the heavens are mourning, too, for these precious lost lives. I am crying also for what my dad went through as a young man, as he says he cries for today's young soldiers.

Before leaving, I stop at the gift shop and get Dad some souvenirs of the *Arizona*. They are doing a booming business here, making me wonder how many other fathers out there have lived a similar story.

My father is finally getting better. His descent into despair has flattened out, and he seems to have his seizures under control. But he is stubborn and doesn't always take his medicine. He is also drinking less, and his lips, once loosened to me by liquor, have tightened up again as taut as a blanket on a military cot awaiting morning inspection.

And now that I am finally listening—now that I am, in fact, taking notes when he rattles on about the "The War"—my dad seems to have less interest in talking. Isn't that just like a jarhead?

Alleyway in an ancient souk, Fez, Morocco

Bad Day in Morocco

Tom Wilmer

I am not a golfer, but, when I received an invitation from King Mohammed VI of Morocco to attend the annual King Hassan II Pro-Am Golf Tournament as one of six North American journalists, how could I refuse?

This was the real deal—a *formal* invitation which arrived in the mail from the king's American press agents, topped with an official, royal Islamic star, a gold seal and fancy French calligraphy. A week later, first-class tickets arrived for passage from JFK to Marrakech aboard a chartered Royal Air Maroc Boeing 747.

The first inkling that this journey would be an out-of-the-ordinary experience occurred just prior to liftoff. With drinks in hand, people casually strolled the aisles—it was cocktail-party central in first class. Some (myself included) sat on armrests talking to pro and amateur golfer seatmates. A large linen-draped trolley, topped with a bouquet of fresh flowers, graced the front of the cabin.

There was no pre-flight safety announcement, no directives to stow your tray tables, buckle up, bring your seat-back up, extinguish your laptop and mobile phone. The flight attendants blithely ambled about, champagne flutes on trays as the turbines roared to full military power. The behemoth 747 rotated, and we were airborne. Hardly anyone was seat-belted. As the craft nosed skyward, we watched amusedly as the flower-cart careened madly down the aisle.

After landing in Marrakech, we were whisked straight

through customs without a moment's pause for suitcase inspections. We were guests of the king. Curbside, two buses awaited, along with police motorcycle and squad car escorts.

Wherever we went during our 10-day stay, a security detachment clung close to the buses, along with plain-clothes secret service agents, Ahmed, one of King Mohammed VI's senior agents and I became instant buddies. A couple even commented that they thought he was my older brother.

Every day, primarily for the golf widows' entertainment, bus excursions were offered to historic destinations such as Casablanca, Fez, Tangiers and the Caves of Hercules. Each morning, as I'd enter La Mamounia Hotel's lobby after breakfast, there was Ahmed, dapper and professional-looking, but with a gracious smile of welcome. He'd approach, put his arm around my shoulder or hold my hand and ask, "Where you go today, Tom?"

I'd then inquire about his bus escort assignment. If I liked the sound of his trip better than my pick, I'd hop on Ahmed's bus. It was a relationship where it wasn't the content or the intensity of conversation that made the friendship special, it was the unspoken, intangible elements. You know, that comfortable sense you instantly get from certain people just met— the feeling that you might have been best buddies in a past life or at least a confident sense of knowing them from somewhere, sometime, long, long ago? That's the way it was with Ahmed and me.

One day, following the entourage's relocation to Rabat, I joined Ahmed's group for a visit to Fez. As we walked through the narrow alleyways of an ancient *souk*, I sensed a particularly scary-looking, bearded man with tattered clothes and a worn-out, grease-stained baseball cap. We'd round a corner in the donkey dung-littered marketplace, and there was the mutant, slithering once again, amidst the crowd. Later in the afternoon, I observed one of the suits whispering clandestinely to the freaky guy and that's when I realized he was one of Ahmed's moles.

One particularly warm afternoon in Rabat, Ahmed approached me in the hotel lobby. He asked if I'd like to go with him as he escorted Noreen, the mother of the pro from Cork, Ireland, and an ultra-wealthy Mexican couple, attending as amateur golfers, to one of Rabat's medina marketplaces. "Sure," I said, "I'll grab my camera and meet you at your car."

Ahmed careened his frog-shaped Citroën at high speeds through the streets of Rabat, whipping the steering wheel about with casual abandon. Our journey was serenaded by the slow, methodical chants of the muezzins' evening calls to the faithful. Competing chants emanated from tinny loudspeakers mounted atop dozens of neighborhood minarets. Inside the walled medina, the atmosphere was festive but relaxed, as locals shopped for the ingredients for their evening meals. The market brimmed with carpets piled high, fresh and dried fruits, oranges and lemons, glistening brassware, silk scarves and leather goods, along with daggers and Bedouin swords dangling from the facades of the open-air stalls.

Ahmed was a master haggler and knew well the real value of the goods being tendered. I discovered this as I started to hand a shopkeeper a $20 bill for a curved Bedouin dagger. Ahmed held my hand back and barked out a few Arabic utterances. He then turned to me and said with a checkmate grin, "The shopkeeper says he will accept eight dollars."

One shop in particular caught my attention with its array of glistening hammered tin and brassware. At the rear of the shop, seated on a tattered stool, sat an elderly man—he looked exactly like the model guy for Zig-Zag rolling papers. Another man, in his thirties, puffed peacefully on a hookah. I wanted to take a picture but thought it prudent to ask Ahmed first since both men would be prominent in the shot. "Yes, of course. No problem. You shoot!"

As I clicked off three or four frames, the Zig-Zag man smiled faintly while the young guy just stared blankly, but then quickly yanked his face away from the lens. As he did so, I noticed an iciness to his gaze.

We walked on and turned a corner in a narrow corridor of the open-air section, all of it looking a bit like the market-place in "Raiders of the Lost Ark." Most everyone we encountered looked peaceful, going about their business serenely, but there were a few whose behavior and expressions raised little alarms in my head. Still, I gaffed it all off as cultural differences. But that's not how my travel-mate, Ms. Noreen from Cork interpreted the situation. This was her first journey Beyond the Pale. By all outward appearances, she was remarkably relaxed, but, now, when I turned to ask her how she was doing, she was semi-paralytic.

"Noreen, are you alright?" I asked.

"No, I don't think so," she announced meekly. "Is it safe here, Tom? Are you sure it's ok?" Her voice had a quavering, bird-like Celtic lilt.

"Of course it is, Noreen!" I answered confidently.

I turned to Ahmed for reassurance, "Ahmed, tell Noreen how safe it is here."

Ahmed stood at attention as he looked in Noreen's eyes and proudly proclaimed in a fatherly tone, "Noreen, I could leave you two here at midnight and I assure you, nothing bad would happen!"

Not more than a minute later, Ahmed turned to me and said, "Tom, if you excuse me for a moment, I should like to go talk to my friend in a shop over there."

Ahmed stepped into a glass-fronted stall a few feet away, and we caught snippets of his pantomime conversation with his friend the local date and almond specialist.

As I turned to comfort Noreen, a curly black-haired man, who walked with a scrunch and looked very much like a severely pissed-off Groucho Marx on LSD, roared straight up to me. He looked at my camera with pure hatred, pointed at my chest, and then glared at me as he waggled his index finger in my face, "You have camera! I have gun! I come back and shoot you in face!" whereupon he vaporized into the crowd of peaceful, fez-capped, caftan-draped, and burka-shrouded late afternoon shoppers.

Not more than 10 seconds later, Ahmed reappeared. He sensed something was akilter. He glanced at me and asked, "Is everything alright?"

"No, Ahmed, actually it's turning out to be a rather shitty day. A guy just walked up and threatened to shoot me. He just ran off, I think, to go get his gun!"

"Where is he? Where'd he go? We get him!" Ahmed said commandingly. He then wrapped his arm through mine and jerked me from a standstill to a full-tilt-boogie.

Instantly, everything went into hyper-drive—a whizzing, whirring, panoramic blur. It was like I had just become the lens of a video camera filming my own Technicolor Hollywood action movie. Card tables overturned, shoppers and peddlers dove out of Ahmed's way as we weaved and dodged down the medina's narrow alleyways—all the time, his right arm tightly interlocked with my left. Ahmed charged ahead like a linebacker bulldozing the defense, and I, the reluctant linebacker sidekick. As we hurtled on toward what seemed a rendezvous with doom, I thought to myself, "This is absurd. Here I am being towed by Ahmed toward the very guy who wants to shoot me, and I'm the only one in my movie without a gun."

Still, somehow, I wasn't scared. The whole situation was unfurling way too fast for that, and it was all way too surreal. Just then, up ahead, I spotted Groucho turning a corner.

"There he is, Ahmed!"

Seconds later, Ahmed tackled the guy, lifted him up by the collar of his olive-drab army jacket. He held him aloft with feet dangling in space as Ahmed rapid-fire rattled off nasty-sounding, spittle-charged Arabic utterances. To complete the scene, imagine about 75 timid, incredulous, mouse-like shoppers standing around us in a tightly packed circle, much like spectators watching a junior-high lunchtime fight. Ahmed then drop-kicked Groucho to the ground, pulled out his glistening, golden king-badge in one hand and pistol in the other. He shoved them alternately in front of the mutant's face as he continued berating him. I imagined that the gist of Ahmed's lecture was something akin to, "You imbecile. You fool! You knave! How could you have insulted a guest of King Mohammed the Sixth? Do you realize how easily you could be shot for such an offense?"

As Groucho lay covered in dust at Ahmed's feet, with an expression that was scared shitless but still pissed off, Ahmed turned to me and said, "How you say in English, I think he is just loco—crazy, but harmless. If it is alright with you, we let him go."

What the hell was I supposed to say? "No, Ahmed, I do not think so. Shoot him!" Instead, I replied, "It is entirely up to you."

Ahmed pulled Groucho up off the ground, dusted him off and sent him scurrying off through the medina's narrow passageway.

And that's the last I saw of Groucho until we were close to the market's two-story, keyhole-arched entrance. I happened to glance into the Zig-Zag guy's stall, and there Groucho was, slightly disheveled and dusty, and obviously still severely pissed off. Lurking in the back of the copper pot-and-pan and dagger shop, he stared out at me with utter, undiluted contempt.

I felt like calling out, "Dude, you started it." But I just turned away, and we walked back to Ahmed's car for the ride back to the Rabat Hilton where we would don tuxedos and join the king's old friend, the golf legend Billy Casper, and his entourage, as they celebrated Casper's birthday with a feast of mutton and entertainment by horn-blaring and tambourine-rattling Bedouin tribesmen.

Jackson Lake, Wyoming

MASTER CLASS

We asked the longtime former travel editor of the *San Francisco Examiner*'s travel section, Georgia Hesse, to single out three submissions to this book for praise, giving one a prize in her name and two others honorable mentions. Although down with a broken hip and, anyway, shut in by COVID, she did so, meeting the deadline we'd set in plenty of time. She also supplied three of her own greatest hits, which we take pleasure in reprinting, noting, in her cover letter, how much humor can contribute to a travel piece.

A longtime friend Don George, her successor as travel editor at the *Examiner,* who went on to become a renowned travel writer and editor in his own right, kindly wrote up an appreciation of her and her legacy. For those who have not met her, his piece gives a vivid sense of Ms. Hesse, as he calls her in his first, nerve-wracking phone interview with her.

It also details the qualities he admires in her work, with the three travel essays that follow giving ample evidence of those qualities. These three take her to Macau, before and after the Chinese take-over, to the North Pole, bundled up so she looks like, she says, Bibendum, the Michelin Man, and to the rainforests of Borneo, in the wake of the American moon landing—the timing of that visit matters, you'll see. Together, they constitute something of a master class in the art and craft of travel writing. They're also time capsules from a heroic era in this field. It was a period when, for a talented editor and writer like her, the world laid itself out, like an oyster on the half shell.

A Toast to Georgia Hesse

Don George

The first time I met Georgia Hesse, I almost fainted. Twice.

The year was 1980. I was an unknown, fledgling free-lance travel writer at the time, and Georgia was the legendary founding Travel Editor of the *San Francisco Examiner*, the grande dame who presided over the paper's thick, award-winning Sunday Travel Section.

I had recently moved to the Bay Area and, like dozens of writers, had submitted an article on spec to the Examiner Travel Section. When I hadn't heard from the section after a few months, I plucked up my courage, picked up the phone and dialed the Travel Section number.

I was expecting a receptionist or editorial assistant to answer. So I was completely unprepared when the phone was picked up and a distinguished voice said, "Georgia Hesse."

That's when I almost fainted.

I managed to recover enough to stutter, "H-h-hello, Ms. Hesse. You-you-you don't know me, but my name is Don George and I sent you a story on Kyushu in Japan and I'm just wondering what the status of the story is."

I'll never forget her response. "I don't know anything about your story," she said, "but I've just been talking with someone about you, and I'd like to meet you. Can you come to the *Examiner*?"

That was the second time I almost fainted.

As it turned out, Georgia was good friends with a writer I had just met on a press trip to Japan. Georgia was planning to take a one-year leave of absence from the paper, and half an hour earlier, she had called that friend to see if she might be interested in taking her place for the year.

"I can't, I'm too busy," the friend had apparently replied, "but I just met a nice young man who recently moved to the Bay Area, and he might be perfect for the job."

Incredibly enough, that was how I ended up working at the *San Francisco Examiner*, first as a Travel Writer and eventually as Travel Editor.

So it is no exaggeration when I say that Georgia Hesse changed my life.

At my first in-person meeting with Georgia, I was enchanted, and happily, she liked me, too. She arranged for me to meet with the publisher and then with the editor and the managing editor, and with her enthusiastic support, I was hired to replace her while she traveled and wrote on her one-year leave.

As soon as I was hired, Georgia took me under her wing—the best wing imaginable for a fledgling travel writer-editor.

My first impression was that Georgia seemed to know just about everything, and whenever she didn't know something, she knew where to go to learn it—an essential art in those pre-Internet days. She was wonderfully worldly, having studied in France as a college student and then having traveled around the globe for two decades as the paper's travel editor.

Over time, I came to know her and her work better, and realized just how exceptional she was as a writer. She had a special talent for bringing places, people and experiences to life with an alchemical mix of erudition, humor, compassion and eloquence, as well as a wizardly way of layering her stories with historical and cultural lessons without a trace of pedantry.

Not all great writers are great editors, or vice versa, but Georgia was also an extraordinarily incisive editor, who brought two essential but rarely combined skills to her work: She was adept at the big-picture organizing of a nationally important Sunday section, that sought to cover the entire world geographically and thematically each week; and she was skilled in the art of story-editing, both refining the larger structure of a piece and fine-tuning sentence by sentence and word by word.

Finally, she was an exemplary ambassador for the newspaper and for the fields of travel writing and publishing. She moved through the world with the same high intelligence, integrity and humor that graced her writing, and she was universally respected and admired. When Georgia walked into a room at any travel-related gathering, every head would turn and you could hear the whispers, "That's Georgia Hesse!"

Back in those halcyon days of the late 1970s and early 1980s, San Francisco was still one of the dominant outposts in the United States for foreign tourism representatives. There were two dozen national government tourism offices in the city at that time, and, every December, they would sponsor a glittering celebration in a grandly decorated hotel ballroom, with a sumptuous, multi-course feast. All of the tourism officials would be there, as well as all of the major Northern California travel writers and editors, both staff and freelance.

At the beginning of that feast, every year, Georgia would

rise from her seat at one end of the ballroom and walk with a slow, queenly dignity past all the festive tables to a podium at the other end of the room. There she would take the stage and bless the gathering with a few choice words that perfectly expressed the essence of the year, the bonhomie of the occasion and the good fortune that we all had to be members of the best industry in the world, in the best city on the planet.

At the end of her one-year leave, we all expected Georgia to resume her position at the paper, but, as it turned out, she was having too much fun to return. Instead, she decided to devote her days to traveling, writing and living well, as she has continued to do ever since.

As for me, I ended up working at the *Examiner* for 15 years, then moved on to other publications and roles, but remarkably, I was able to build my entire professional career on the foundation of that one year working as a writer and editor in Georgia's stead.

Looking back to that time now, I feel lucky beyond words to have had Georgia as my mentor. When I took her place, the Examiner Travel Section was considered one of the very top travel sections in the country, and she was a legend among her fellow editors and among her readers, who were devoted to her Sunday columns and tales. She was beloved for bringing the world into Northern California homes every weekend with stories—her own and others—that infused travels near and far with an engaging, inspiring sense of wonder and fun.

Georgia did her best to teach me, by word and by example, how to edit a complex and conspicuous Sunday section, how to treat fellow writers and editors graciously, how to honor readers and how to construct the intricate weekly puzzle of a world-covering publication for a sophisticated and passionate audience.

What a role model! Georgia was—and still is—the consummate travel writer and editor, the exemplar of a kind that's increasingly hard to find, who works hard and plays hard and loves with an equal passion both the world and the word.

Looking back over the spectacular span of her career, I realize that I have learned more from her, and am more grateful to her, than I can ever adequately express.

And I realize too how profoundly her writing and her editing have enriched all of our days and have made us all better, deeper human beings.

Thinking of all this, I picture her now in my mind. She is sitting regally at the end of an enormous, festively decorated ballroom. That room is filled with all of her fans, writers and readers and industry leaders. Georgia surveys the room and smiles, and a hush falls over the scene. Then all as one, we rise, turn her way and lift our glasses of champagne. And speaking for us all, I look at her and say: "This is for you, dear Georgia. You are truly one of a kind, and we all feel blessed beyond measure to have you in our lives."

Night Boat to Macau

Georgia Hesse

When I was the Dragon Lady, Queen of the South China Sea, I was tall and willowy, dressed all in white and wore a dagger in my garter. I operated out of an opium den in *Macau*, the wickedest port in the world.

That was when I was 12 years old, not incidentally. Macau was out of Rudyard Kipling and Noel Coward, out of Robert Louis Stevenson and "Terry and the Pirates," the seemingly eternal Milton Caniff cartoon strip. I didn't know what opium was, but it sounded swell. So did the name Macau: mysterious, dissolute, delightful.

It seems that once Macau may have been as villainous as I wanted it to be. Dutch author Hendrick de Leeuw in his *Cities of Sin* (1934) painted it in the purplest of proses: Macau "harbors in its hidden places the riffraff of the world, the drunken shipmasters, the flotsam of the sea, the derelicts, and more beautiful, savage women than any port in the world. It is a hell." Heaven.

Many years ago, on my first visit as an adult, I spurned whatever speedy transportation existed from Hong Kong (40 wave-tossed miles away) in favor of the "night boat to Macau." That sounded more romantic but was just more tawdry, a case that frequently occurs. I stayed at the then new Hotel Lisboa, a gaudy confection where gambling (the *sine qua non* of Macau's economic life) went on 24 hours a day. (Macau came under China's control in December, 1999, and gaming returned to the island in 2002. Today, there are more than 30 casinos; it's a maxi-Vegas.)

Away from the garishness and the games tables (craps, roulette, blackjack, baccarat in addition to the Chinese *dai siu* and *fan tan* and the slot machines, in ever-descriptive Chinese, known as "hungry tigers"), I found the city sad and scruffy, the only tone of faded colonial splendor sounding at the creaky old inn, the Bela Vista.

Early in the '90s, I found myself crossing from Hong Kong to Macau again, this time aboard a jetfoil that streaked across the 40 miles in 55 minutes. (There were other vessels available: jetcats, jumbocats, hoverferries, high-speed ferries and helicopters, but no more stomach-churning night boats.)

Macau then was living through tremulous, perhaps even parlous days. (I like the ancient Chinese curse: "May you live in interesting times.") It had changed faster during the previous decade than in four centuries under the Portuguese flag.

Macau is the oldest European outpost in Asia, settled between 1554 and 1557 during Portugal's great era of expansion. It's a small peninsula dangling off the belly of China, south of Guangzhou (Canton) and two small islands in the Pearl River Delta, Taipa and Coloane, to which it is joined by bridges.

The Portuguese jewel grew rich from the China-Europe trade and became the summer home of the British *taipans* (big traders). But in 1841, when the Brits established Hong Kong as a trading Crown Colony, Macau slipped into a languid backwater, a free port (since 1846) where tourists and Hong Kong residents came to shop (particularly for gold) and to gamble.

They also came to eat, to drink inexpensive Portuguese wines (such as the estimable Dão) and to disport themselves, enjoying the good life with bad girls.

For years, Macau slumbered, a lost leaf off the blooming Hong Kong plant. When Ian Fleming, creator of Bond, James Bond, arrived in 1959, he found it "as picturesque as, and deader than, a beautiful graveyard."

In 1992, I found Macau a two-day escape from whatever else I was doing then; a look back in nostalgia. The reproduction of a brilliantly red 1920s London bus followed a fixed route along the more touristy streets, emblazoned with a sign reading "For the Cordialities Showing Oriental Elegance." I began again at the very real beginning, A-Ma Temple, to pay respects to the Taoist goddess of seafarers.

One day, long ago (most happenings if not all in Macau were long ago), a junk sailing across the South China Sea found itself trapped and battered by a sudden storm. At its height, a beautiful, young woman who had boarded at the last moment rose to command the gale winds and the mad seas to calm. They did, and the ship floated safely into port. The woman (named A-Ma) stepped ashore, walked to the crest of the nearby Barra Hill and ascended into heaven in a halo of light and a waft of perfume.

Centuries later, when Portuguese sailors landed and asked the name of the place, they were told "Am-Ma-Gao" (Bay of A-Ma). Eventually, Amagao became Macau.

Fireworks, the odor of incense from burning joss sticks, a celebration of shrieking children: all these seemed memories of an old, old culture. So did the baroque facade of St. Paul's with its intricate carvings, standing tall since the church itself burned down in 1835. Tourists snapped each other wearing Hawaiian shirts, pretty springtime dresses and T-shirts bearing messages such as "Refresh the Spirit Excellent."

In those days, antique shops near St. Paul's sold precious (one presumed) items from the Chang dynasty (1644-1912) or even Ming (1368-1644) bowls, etc., smuggled out of China. You could touch the past in the Old Protestant Cemetery, where lay Dr. Robert Morrison (compiler of the first English-Chinese dictionary), George Chinnery (doyen of China coast landscape artists in the 18th century) and Capt. Lord John Spencer Churchill (commander of the H.M. *Druid*—an inspired name—and an ancestor of Sir Winston's).

Luiz Vaz de Camoens, soldier-poet who composed the national epic "Os Lusiades" strode here. So did Vasco da Gama, the first European to sail 'round the Cape of Good Hope, and Sun Yat Sen, the founder of the modern Chinese Republic and medical practitioner in Macau.

One had to visit Taipa village on Taipa Island, to eat (to dine would be too formal an act) at the irrepressible Pinocchio's, where the shrimp and the crab seemed to have jumped upon your plate at your beckoning. Fortified, you continued to the isle of Coloane to view the arm bone of St. Francis Xavier in a silver reliquary along with remains of Christian martyrs who died far away in Nagasaki and Indochina—more lively stories.

On its website, I read that "Macau has shifted from being primarily a manufacturing-based economy, with a heavy emphasis on the textiles sector, to becoming a service economy focused heavily ... etc., etc." all that stilted stuff. Stable growth, recovering economy and restoration of public order are concepts tossed about, and a leading attraction is the Cyber Fountain in the Nam Vam Lakes, largest of its kind in Asia, with water jets and music controlled entirely by computer. Clearly, it's a fountain into which the inebriated and unruly dare not jump.

Planes land in the spiffy airport, gliding in over waters innocent of night boats. Days and nights, the city celebrates with youth symphony concerts, puppet shows, women's hockey, children's choirs, string quartets, fireworks competitions and sketching exhibitions at Old Ladies House.

So where will the Dragon Lady linger languorously tomorrow? I doubt she'll be back. Macau is no longer wicked enough.

On Top of the World

Georgia Hesse

WHAM! SMACK! WHACK! Smash! Thud! Shudder-creak-crash! I am nearly seasick in this coffin-sized wooden box as it hammers relentlessly into the ridges of ice atop frozen Barrow Strait. The coffin is sealed upon a *komatik* (an Inuit sled), which is pulled by a snorting Skidoo, and I am buried under a caribou hide that would smell worse than bad drains were it not stiff with icicles.

Icicles have grown over the eye-slits of my goose-down mask, and its rubbery nose is bent to the side, making me suck hard for air. Blood throbs under my toenails, wanting to get out. All my bones ache from the endless pounding. Oh, no; now my sore shoulder bone is itching! An icy wind wails between the wooden slats and pierces through my parka like a jet of needles.

What, O Great Sky Father, am I doing here?

What I was doing was trekking to the North Pole, the real one, the geographic one, the one 1,600 miles north of the Arctic Circle, the one where Santa Claus lives and eats blubber for breakfast; what can I say?

The North Pole is not a usual destination; I had been told I would certainly be among the first dozen women to set foot there. It is a lonely abstraction, the coldest of calculations. It calls because it is there, and only the mad answer. (As expedition leader, Mike Dunn had told his eight adventurers that first night in Alberta, "All of you have a screw loose. But it is the right screw.")

While I was stretched in my coffin, we thumped across Barrow Strait from Resolute on Cornwallis Island to Beechey Island. Scheduled as a five-hour slide, it became instead an 11-hour ride aboard a battering ram. Storms had whipped the ice into upthrusts called pressure ridges on which the Skidoos skidded and coughed and our sleds faltered; nothing for it but to rise (miserably) from my coffin to help push.

Was I clumsy? Also lubberly and, face it, fat. I owed that (but also my life, I now know) to the outfitters of High Arctic International Explorer Service back in Resolute. I had felt stuffed as a sausage even before Resolute, squeezed into two sets of long underwear (one silk, one wool), ski pants, ski mitts, ski sweater, lined parka, socks in silk and socks in wool, feet encased in those Canadian Caribou boots that have stiff liners inside *them*. Then, in Resolute, we were swaddled in U.S. military-inspired outer Arctic gear: thick powder-pants, parkas with fur-rimmed hoods, all-obscuring down masks, mittens larger than Yogi Berra's catcher's mitt. I could scarcely toddle; I looked like Bibendum, the Michelin Man.

(What a joy and a coincidence to look up "clumsy" in the dictionary and to discover it descends from the Middle English "clumsen," to be stiff with cold.)

As I slogged over the ridges, I remembered a conversation with my ophthalmologist: "And will my contact lenses freeze at the Pole?" I had asked. "Not," he answered with a grin, "until your eyes do."

"Well, now," I thought in my best Pollyanna manner, "let's consider something pleasant." Like what? Like the Englishman of the Adolphus W. Greely expedition who hacked off his own feet to avoid gangrene? Like James

Fitzjames of the fated Sir John Franklin party (of the happily named ships *Erebus* and *Terror*) who wintered *right near here* in 1845-46 and watched his wretched comrades perish, only then to give up his own ghost? Nice going.

I heard somebody else's voice in the almost tangible cold. "Mush, you huskies," it said.

Eventually, at 3:05 a.m., we spotted pointy Italian tents on the windswept beach of Beechey. We staggered, we tottered, we stripped off the few top layers and plopped down, asleep in our bags on the snow. Unlike Franklin, we were rescued next day by Twin Otters and flown back to Resolute in about 40 minutes, where we careened into the Arctic Circle Club bar.

In late afternoon, our Twin Otters skied down upon Lake Hazen, Ellesmere Island, about 1,200 miles north of the Arctic Circle, where a giant, rubber quonset hut served as dormitory. Pilot Harry Hanlan radioed to a remote weather station. Crackles coming back told him the situation was fine, and we should make our attempt for the Pole very soon. We flew off, refueled at Tanquary Fjord, and headed up the 70th meridian for the 560-mile push to the Pole.

It was twilight when we crossed the last headland of the North American continent and roared out over the Arctic Ocean. We were to land where there is no land.

The Arctic is a crinkled, white desert cut by pressure ridges and studded with ice islands (not icebergs) unique to the Arctic; the first two discovered were larger than Guam.

At 2:11 a.m., in the noon-bright light, we landed at 89.07 degrees latitude and stepped out of the Otter, smack (well, 90 degrees is smack) on top of the world. My heart threatened to beat itself away. Burdened with cameras and my own bulk,

I clambered out of the plane into the white-glaring light, somehow managing to step on my sunglasses, then sticking them sideways in front of my tired eyes. I looked like a loony.

What does one do at the Pole? First, I tried to find a bathroom behind a pressure ridge. My fingers refused entirely to rezip my Arctic pants and, as I looked up toward our little plane, the pilot was standing on the wing, doubled over, laughing.

So what else does one *do* at the Pole? We did something neither Peary nor Cook accomplished, that was not contemplated by Fridtjof Nansen or Roald Amundsen or even Prince Luigi Amedeo of Savoy, Duke of Abruzzi. Raising the candy-striped pole we had brought along, we popped open bottles of Mumm's Cordon Rouge and downed it before it could turn into slush.

I toppled over and sang "Sittin' on Top of the World." From me, all directions stretched south.

At 7:18 a.m., we skied down again at Hazen and spotted the tracks of wolves that had lapped around our camp during the long night. Carried away with the courage of conquerors, we feasted on Arctic char caught through the lake ice, drank Scotch chilled with pieces of glacier (Scotch-and-Snowda), and so to bed.

The temperature sank and the winds whipped up, and, as I snuggled into my sleeping bag, I wondered whether anything would ever be exciting again.

I needn't have worried. Winging from our Lake Hazen base south to Grise Fjord on the south tip of Ellesmere Island, we looked down upon solitary peaks poking up like frozen islands adrift in an Arctic snow-sea.

The town of Grise, a struggle of houses along the ice-bound sea, is the northernmost non-military settlement in the world and home of 111 independent souls, most of them Innu who survive largely on a subsistence, hunting economy. Nearly every household owns at least one Skidoo.

The call of the wild has a peculiar power over some psyches. "Who wants to sleep in an igloo?" Mike inquired one noon over lunch in the perfectly adequate prefab that serves as the Grise Fjord Lodge. I raised my hand. It was the only one.

"Fraidy cats," I thought, and looked expectantly towards our pilots. "No way," confessed John Brechin, or maybe it was Peter Milne. "I got a good, warm bed in there." Both eyed me warily, as if I had become unhinged.

Later, in the fading light of 11 p.m. that serves as the summer's poor excuse for darkness, I waddled out over the sea ice toward the igloo and bellied inside its low entrance. I stripped down to long underwear and slid into my well-chilled bag. Dunn, photographer Wolfgang Kaehler and a teacher who was passing through town (why?) decided to join in the adventure. Dunn had brought Scotch and Kahlua as icebreakers.

Sleeping was OK; waking at 6 a.m. and scurrying out of my bag cocoon into the chrysalis of the igloo at a temperature of 11 degrees below zero was not. My fingers tried with only partial success to dress me; they refused entirely to touch the heavy zippers of the outside Arctic pants or to tighten themselves around the laces of my boots. As decently clothed as they would permit, I stumbled-ran back across the ice toward the small hotel that looked, suddenly, like Italy's Villa d'Este.

There was, as it happened, no hot water in the hotel that morning (fortunately, coffee had been made before the power gave out), so I washed my contact lenses in melted snow and tried to think how some brave Brits subsisted on sea birds, ptarmigan, foxes, seals and algae through a bleak, black winter 250 days long

Amazing how much better one feels when contemplating the catastrophes of others.

It is over. I have traveled poles apart and now can put both feet on the table after dinner. (Jeannette Mirsky began her *To the Arctic!* thus: "Not so long ago there was a custom among sailors that accorded to all those who had sailed around Cape Horn the right to put one foot on the table after dinner, while those who had crossed the Arctic could put both feet on the table.") First one big Caribou boot and then the other.

—⚏— —⚏— —⚏— —⚏—

Addendum: A year following the Pole adventure, I found myself aboard the good ship *Lindblad Polaris* outward bound from Dakar, Senegal, for an exploration of mostly remote West Africa. A writer on board was Jack Schnedler, then travel editor of the *Chicago Sun-Times*. My best buddies included Bruce Hamby of the *Denver Post*.

"Let's have first-night drinks in my cabin," Bruce offered. "You don't want smokers in yours." Right. So we invited the five or six other writers on board.

"God!" Jack remarked as we were introduced. "You've been everywhere."

I, modestly: "Well, not quite."

Jack, eagerly: "Well, maybe not. I can tell you one place you've never been. The North Pole."

I, with unaccustomed prescience: "Hm-m-m-m." (Neither Bruce nor any other friend blurted.)

Jack: "Let me tell you something. I've got the most fantastic picture with a press release from Society Expeditions. It's from a trip to the North Pole." (We sat, silent, waiting for him to dig his own hole.) "There are these weird-looking people and a silly striped pole and in the middle is a fat, goggle-eyed, middle-aged sherry-drinker who couldn't care less where she is–or may not know." (We all listened to the shovel-shovel of the dig.)

Jack, unstoppable: "Wonderful! I would just love to know who she was. Poor thing."

I allowed a theatrical silence before I spoke. "C'était moi," I intoned.

No gasp, no choke. Jack turned as gray-white and wrinkled as a pressure ridge. He left and we didn't see him until the next afternoon.

Would you believe we are now friends?

Big Man Go Moon

Georgia Hesse

As a child, I knew three dates in July worth celebration: July 4, 1776, anniversary of the American Declaration of Independence; July 8, our mother's birthday; and July 14, 1789, Bastille Day, the birthday (as conceived ever since) of *la belle France.*

In 1969, I found another one: July 20, when America's Apollo 11, crewed by Neil Armstrong, Buzz Aldrin and Michael Collins, made the first lunar landing. "One small step for a man; one giant leap for mankind!" said Armstrong to an earthly audience. With that, the Space Age debuted.

A few days later, squished into a very small aircraft, I was winging above the wild, green peaks of the Owen Stanley Range, the spine of Papua New Guinea. I gazed down on tangled wilderness sliced by the Sepik, the Strickland and the Fly Rivers; down and back into the Stone Age.

Incredibly, only 36 years before, Europeans had first penetrated that damp, shadowed world to find in its deep valleys not gold but unknown, uncounted human beings. Separated by serrated mountains like teeth on an endless saw, these people had dwelt for thousands of years in isolated, tribal groups, unaware of each other, speaking 860 languages. Today, three of them are "official": English, Tok Tisin (Pidgin, a creole tongue) and Hisi Motu.

Off the insect-sized airplane, I stepped into a frontier fling, the Saturday market day of Mt. Hagan, still swinging after its annual *sing-sing* (festival). Near-naked male dancers who had walked for weeks to show off here straggled through the throng, their waists bound by wide belts of beaten bark from which dangled brief fabrics (in front) and bunches of tanet grass (behind).

"'Morrow," said my Australian guide, "we'll find a *sing-sing*. Ready at dawn, right?" Right.

Hot, hot morning when it came, even before the clear, broiling globe of sun had climbed above the peak-points. High grass, dirt road and, on the green-brown plain below, dozens and then hundreds of men and woman paraded, brilliant plumes flouncing on heads, the priceless feathers of birds of paradise. "Kah-mon an' walk behind me, yeah?"

In a green bower, a crone huddled, old eyes running, flinty shoulders slumped, cheeks sunk beyond sharp bones, legs below the knees ash-gray from cooking fires, ancient hooked nose painted red: antiquity still living. "How old is she?" I whispered. "Probably 35," answered my guide. I nearly dropped my Nikon. It was my 36th birthday.

Days drifted. In the Eastern Highlands, we encountered a mass of Mudmen, horrible yet humorous in their sooty skins and great mud masks shaped liked eccentric eggs. A young man leaned on his stick. We greeted him in Pidgin. The warrior pierced me with his eyes. "Who bilong him?" he asked. (In Pidgin, both sexes are "him.")

The Aussie drew a long track in the dirt. "Faraway, faraway," he almost sang. "Him," pointing at me, "Him bilong America!" The tribesman's eyes expanded until they filled his face: wonder, awe, a bit of fear. "*Him?*" he questions. "Him bilong America big man go moon?"

I got it. Through TV magic, this warrior from the Mountains of Heaven had watched from the Stone Age into space as a man named America flew to the moon. And I bilonged him. I felt very proud.

Acknowledgments

I would like to thank the volunteers who helped put this anthology together, including those who joined me on the small committee moving this project from concept to publication. They are, in alphabetical order, Jim Gebbie, Judith Horstman, Karen Misuraca and Amy Sherman.

Jim oversaw the submissions process. With his customary efficiency and diplomacy, he ensured entries were judged blind, keeping the identity of all submitters a secret, both from the judges and the other committee members. Judith, in her capacity as president of BATW, contributed a thoughtful introduction to this work as well as contributing her creative ideas and general willingness to muck in to all aspects of this project. Karen oversaw all of our interactions with the busy judges, convincing them to review their entries quickly and carefully. In my native Canada, our Senate is supposed to provide sober, second thoughts, after the House of Parliament has put draft legislation forward. Amy played that role on our committee—her judgment was an asset to the project throughout.

We are also thankful to the judges who donated their time to review the submissions for this anthology—their names and bios are printed on page 177. Of these, we are particularly grateful to Don George, Catharine Hamm and Georgia Hesse for also contributing, *pro bono*, their considerable talents as writers to this volume. Catharine wrote a short prologue to the book, contributing some necessarily tentative ideas about where travel writing might go from here (see page xi). In a section we've called Master Class (beginning at page 154), the renowned travel writer and editor Don George introduces readers to the class's leader, the inimitable Georgia Hesse, the former editor of the *San Francisco Examiner*'s travel section. After that, we've selected three of Georgia's greatest hits by way of showing (not telling) how it's done.

Bob Cooper was the book's chief copy editor, casting an eagle eye over much of the text, communicating his queries to contributors with care, smoothing out rough patches and catching errors throughout. My thanks to you, Bob—and, for assistance in vetting the copy, to committee members Amy, Jim and Judith.

Our heartfelt appreciation goes to the publishing (and life) team of Jim Shubin and Laurie McAndish King, both longtime members of BATW. Among many other tasks, they laid out the book and designed its cover, dealt with all our image submissions, secured an ISBN number and made arrangements for distribution of the print and digital versions of the book. They have overseen the publication of all six BATW books to date. We're so very grateful to them for offering up, again, their time, energy and expertise on our behalf.

—*Alec Scott*
BATW Board Member
and Book Committee Chair

Process for Selecting Submissions and Awarding Prizes

Two judges reviewed each pseudonymous entry, giving each piece a rating from 1 to 10. If the average of these two ratings was higher than 7.5 out of a possible 10, it was accepted for publication. Those with the highest ratings were then forwarded to judge Catharine Hamm, who devised a shorter list of pieces, which were, in turn, submitted to Georgia Hesse. She then singled out the top three pieces to receive prizes in her name.

Judges' Bios

Sivani Babu is the cofounder, co-CEO and Creative Director of the exploration-driven magazine *Hidden Compass*. An award-winning journalist and nature photographer, she has contributed to *BBC Travel*, *AFAR, Backpacker* and *Outdoor Photographer*. Her work has been recognized in the Best American Travel Writing series, and images have been exhibited from San Diego to the Sorbonne. A former federal public defender, she represented hundreds of indigent defendants. She has chased storms through Tornado Alley, searched for polar bears in the Arctic Circle and navigated the Bermuda Triangle using only the planets and stars. Babu is currently working on her first book, *Saving the Night: Shedding Light on the Importance of Darkness.*

Karen Benke is the author of *Ripe the Page* (translated into Chinese, Korean and Russian) and *Write Back Soon: Adventures in Letter Writing*, among other titles for children and adults. A writing guide for more than 30 years, she directs Creative Writing Adventures, a nonprofit program of Cal-Poets, and leads writing adventures in the San Francisco Bay Area, and in Florence, Italy, at the Numeroventi Design Center. She is currently finishing a picture book in English and Italian.

Nancy Day is a widely published journalist, former Associated Press editor and professor. She has been Journalism Chair and Associate Professor of Journalism at Columbia College Chicago and Director of Advanced Journalism Studies at Boston University, and she was a Nieman fellow at Harvard and a Fulbright fellow in Russia.

Don George has been the travel editor at the *San Francisco Examiner/Chronicle*, founder and editor of Salon.com's Wanderlust and global travel editor for Lonely Planet. He is currently editor at large for *National Geographic Travel*. Don is the author of *The Way of Wanderlust: The Best Travel-Writing of Don George* and *How to Be a Travel Writer*, the bestselling travel writing guide in the world. In addition to writing and editing, Don leads tours, teaches writing workshops, and speaks and consults around the globe. He is cofounder and chair of the acclaimed Book Passage Travel Writers & Photographers Conference.

Don Gibbons was editor-in-chief at *Medical World News* and Director of Communications at Stanford University Medical Center. While at Stanford, serving as editor of *Stanford Medicine* magazine, the publication was awarded the Sibley award for best university magazine. During his long career, he was also Associate Dean for Public Affairs at Harvard Medical School and Chief Communications Officer for the California Institute for Regenerative Medicine.

John Greenman is the Carolyn McKenzie and Don E. Carter Distinguished Professor of Journalism at the University of Georgia's Grady College of Journalism and Mass Communication, and the author of Introduction to Travel Journalism: On the Road with Serious Intent. He was editor, publisher and corporate officer for Knight Ridder, where he helped lead a team that won the Pulitzer Prize. Greenman has reported from 25 countries on five continents.

Jeff Greenwald is the founder of Ethical Traveler, a global community supporting human rights and environmental protection. He is also the author of several best-selling books, including *Shopping for Buddhas* and *The Size of the World*. His most recent book, *Out of Nothing*, is a compilation of his conversations with Burning Man founder Larry Harvey. Greenwald is a faculty member of the Book Passage Travel Writers Conference and served as host of the Ethical Traveler Podcast through 2017. He also developed and performed a critically acclaimed solo show, "Strange Travel Suggestions."

Catharine Hamm recently retired from the *Los Angeles Times*, where she served 17 years as travel editor. Hamm has three times received individual Lowell Thomas Awards, and the *Times'* travel section was recognized nine times during her tenure as editor. She is President of the SATW Foundation and is a past president of the SATW (Society of American Travel Writers).

Paul Lasley and **Elizabeth Harryman** produce and host two daily radio shows that are broadcast to a million listeners in 167 countries on the American Forces Network and air on their podcast at OnTravel.com. They have hosted radio shows on KABC and public radio station KPCC, and for Discovery Channel Radio on XM Satellite. Their shows have won two Gold and one Silver Lowell Thomas Travel Journalism awards. Paul and Elizabeth also write the "Travel Smart" column for *Westways*, the magazine of the Auto Club of Southern California, where Elizabeth recently retired after 21 years as travel editor. During her tenure, *Westways* won six Lowell Thomas Travel Journalism awards.

Christine Loomis was the first travel editor at *Parents* magazine and editor-in-chief of two national publications, and her writing and photography have appeared online and in print. A regular contributor to *USA Today 10Best* and *Travel Age West,* she also writes for multiple meetings-industry publications, among others. She's an SATW board member and chair of SATW's Freelance Council. Among her awards is one for an article on human trafficking in the travel industry, and her essays have appeared in two travel anthologies, most recently *Oscar's Dreamland* in *The Best Women's Travel Writing, Vol. 11: True Stories from Around the World* in 2017.

Josephine Matyas is a full-time freelance writer whose words have appeared on the pages of North American magazines, newspapers and websites for more than two decades. She specializes in travel pieces and admits it's a way to feed an addiction to exploring and experiencing new places and meeting interesting people. Matyas never tires of delving into soft outdoor adventure, history, culture, regional music, RV travel and the great outdoors. You can follow her at: writerwithoutborders.com and at travelswithrigby.com.

Contributors' Bios

Lisa Alpine is a renowned dance teacher and travel writer. Her award-winning stories have appeared in many anthologies, including *Best Travel Writing from Travelers' Tales*. (For a selection of her work, go to www.lisaalpine.com.) She is the author of *Dance Life: Movin'* and *Groovin' Around the Globe, Exotic Life: Travel Tales of an Adventurous Woman* and *Wild Life: Travel Adventures of a Worldly Woman*—Foreword Reviews named the latter the best travel book of the year. Alpine divides her time between Mill Valley and the Big Island of Hawaii, where Pele's lava licks at the edges of her writing retreat.

Barbara Barrielle is a longtime publicist-turned-writer. She writes about travel, wine, entertainment, food and lifestyle and has published two books, *99 Things to do in Sonoma County* and *Where did Thaddeus go?: A small, lost dog's journey through the big wonderful world of Los Angeles*. She lives in Healdsburg, where she has a vineyard and has spent her quarantine days renovating a 1967 Airstream. Her favorite places to visit are the South Pacific (especially the Cook Islands), Montana, New York and, of course, California. She writes regularly for *Wine Industry Advisor, The Napa Valley Register, Oregon Wine Press, The East Hampton Star* and *NW Travel and Life*.

Robert W. Bone is widely known for his guidebooks to Hawaii, Australia, New Zealand and Alaska and has been publishing articles and photos for 70 years. He has traveled throughout all seven continents. After working for 13 years for the *Honolulu Daily Advertiser,* he left to set up his own electronic feature service. The longtime member of the Society of American Travel Writers served two years as chairman of its Western Chapter. In 1990, he was recognized as a member of the Journalism Hall of Fame by Bowling Green State University. In 2014, he published *Fire Bone! A Maverick Guide to a Life in Journalism.*

Rosie Cohan has traveled to more than 60 countries, including 25 trips to Turkey, her "home away from home." Her award-winning storytelling brings to life the beauty of the natural world, introduces intriguing characters and explores different cultural traditions. No matter where she travels, she focuses on showing the universality of the human experience. Her stories have been published on the GeoEx.com Wanderlust blog, travelerstales.com and besttravelwriting.com. Also, as an International Management and Organizational Development Consultant, Cohan has published articles in professional magazines and journals. She lives and writes in Berkeley, a world unto itself.

Monica Conrady is a travel and feature writer based in San Francisco. One of the founding members of Bay Area Travel Writers, she has been active in the development of the organization ever since. Originally from London, she has traveled extensively and rarely met a country she didn't like—or didn't like to write about. Along the way, she has worked at the Cannes Film Festival, the Winter Olympics in Grenoble and the headquarters of the first Whitbread Round the World yacht race in Sydney. One of the thrills of her lifetime was dancing in Rio's Carnaval.

Diane Covington-Carter has won awards for her travel writing, photography, NPR commentaries and books. Her articles have appeared in the *Los Angeles Times*, Hemispheres, sierra.com, *Reader's Digest* and *France Today* (among others), and her memoir, *Finding Gilbert, A Promise Fulfilled* (2018), received a Gold Award from the Society of American Travel Writers. She holds American and Australian passports and divides her time between an eight-acre organic apple farm in the foothills of the Sierra and the beaches of Golden Bay, New Zealand.

Lee Daley credits her lifelong passion for in-depth travel to a life-changing, 110-day, round-the-world trip with Semester at Sea aboard the SS *Universe* more than 20 years ago. A founding member and former president of BATW, she remains in love with our world and its people. Widely published and exhibited, her award-winning travel features and photos continue to share that passion. Visit Lee's website/blog at Epicurean Destinations for a taste of her travels: www.epicureandestinations.com.

Laura Deutsch has traveled the world in search of the answers to life's big questions such as, "Why did that guru give me a mantra that's the name of a high-end furniture store?" Along the way, she mastered the Equine Experience to attain enlightenment by grooming a horse. Her adventures and misadventures have entertained readers of the *Los Angeles Times, San Francisco Chronicle, Christian Science Monitor,* and others. She has led writing retreats from Tassajara to Tuscany. Her piece in this anthology, "The Rhythms of Arezzo," is the winner of the inaugural Georgia Hesse Prize for the top story submitted.

Ginger Dingus was bitten by the travel bug in the 1970s when she snagged a college teaching gig on the shipboard Semester at Sea program and now rates ships as her travel mode of choice. During her 30-plus years as a travel writer, she has cruised to the Arctic, Antarctic and up the Amazon. When not cruising the high seas, you'll find Ginger cruising the rails aboard luxury trains. Wherever she travels, she's on the lookout for the local wildlife. Her articles have appeared in outlets including *Porthole, Cruise Travel, World of Cruising, CruiseCritic* and *TravelAge West*.

M. T. Eley is an Ohio-born writer who lives in San Francisco. He enjoys old books, old souls and the occasional old fashioned, and admires Rudyard Kipling and Mark Twain as the finest English-language travel writers. After graduating from Kenyon College in 2015, he spent four years living in five different countries across four continents, generally loitering and collecting his thoughts. Eventually, he settled down in California but suspects that a writer in motion tends to stay in motion. In addition to travel and essay writing, he edits the *East By West*, an online opinions publication with international readership.

Bill Fink is an award-winning writer with credits in more than 50 publications, including the *San Francisco Chronicle, Outside Magazine, AFAR,* Lonely Planet, Yahoo and CNN. He lived for a year in the Philippines, a source for this story and many more misadventures behind a (hopefully) upcoming book called *Dunked in Manila*. Follow his ongoing global travels and stories @finktravels on Twitter and Instagram and at www.billfinktravels.com.

Laurie McAndish King's award-winning essays and photography have appeared in *Smithsonian Magazine, the San Francisco Chronicle, The Best Women's Travel Writing,* Lonely Planet's *The Kindness of Strangers* and other magazines and literary anthologies. Her most recent book, *Your Crocodile Has Arrived: More True Stories from a Curious Traveler,* includes stories about 20-foot-long earthworms, a Brazilian shaman and an Ivy League astrophysicist's explanation of how flying saucers are powered. She also wrote *An Erotic Alphabet,* for which she was dubbed "The Shel Silverstein of Erotica." A story in her first book, *Lost, Kidnapped, Eaten Alive,* won the coveted Lowell Thomas Gold award. Read more at: LaurieMcAndishKing.com.

David A. Laws photographs and writes about travel, the technology pioneers of Silicon Valley and the history of gardens from his home on the Monterey Peninsula. His work has appeared in numerous broadcast, electronic and print media outlets, including the BBC, NPR, *Pacific Horticulture Magazine, Santa Rosa Press Democrat,* and *Eden,* the quarterly journal of the California Garden & Landscape History Society as well as mobile apps and guidebooks.

Diane LeBow has been chloroformed and robbed on an Italian train, ridden a camel through locust swarms on the Libyan Sahara and searched for the descendants of the Amazons among Mongolian horsewomen. Her work has appeared in *Salon, Via, Image, Seal* and Travelers' Tales and is frequently anthologized. (See www.dianelebow.com.) It has won many honors, including 22 Solas Awards and a Lifetime Achievement Award from Douglass College, Rutgers University, for her writing, photojournalism and women's rights work. The holder of one of the first doctorates in Women's Studies from the University of California, she has been a pioneer in this field, introducing courses in it in France, Holland and the U.S.

Carole Terwilliger Meyers is the author of 18 books, including *Miles of Smiles: 101 Great Car Games & Activities*. An award-winning freelance writer, Carole is also a blogger at Travels with Carole (www.travelswithcarole.blogspot.com), the web publisher of Berkeley and Beyond (www.berkeley-andbeyond.com) and a webcam traveler (www.webcam-traveler.com). Carole has been a featured guest on the *Today* show and quoted in *The New York Times* and *The Wall Street Journal*. She has worked as a movie and restaurant critic and is a member of the Society of American Travel Writers and Bay Area Travel Writers.

Effin Older is a writer, photographer, editor and tutor. Her work has appeared in *Hemispheres, The New York Times, The Washington Post, National Geographic Traveler* and *Ski America*. She has published 20 children's books and written and taken the photographs for an adult book, *Snowboarding*. Her photos also appear in *Backroad & Offroad Biking* and *Cross-Country Skiing for Everyone*. With her husband Jules Older, she has created mini-movies with well over 265,000 views at www.YouTube.com/JulesOlder.

Jules Older is hardly a model of constancy. He has been a disc jockey and ditch digger, medical educator and clinical psychologist, TV villain and children's and adult author, travel writer and ski editor, writer and blogger. He's a business consultant and creator of the award-winning course for writers, Writing for Real. His work has won awards in four countries. He lives in two of them—the U.S. and New Zealand.

April Orcutt has written for *BBC Travel, National Geographic Traveler, Travel and Leisure, Hemispheres* and *the San Francisco Chronicle*, among other outlets. She has worked as a columnist for the *Los Angeles Times* and contributed many other pieces to it. She has also written programs for and helped produce two science television series. Orcutt has been nominated for a local Emmy and has won top honors in the U.S. Travel Association's IPW Awards, Visit California's Eureka! Awards and the Lowell Thomas Travel Journalism Competition. Her piece in this anthology, *Tibetan Bargain with a Twist*, is a recipient of a Georgia Hesse Prize, honorable mention.

Donna Peck launched her travel-writing career with *Romantic Days and Nights in San Francisco*, the first title in Globe Pequot's award-winning series. In her 30-year career, Peck's work has been featured in *Cathay Pacific, Coastal Living, Preservation, Global Traveler* and *San Francisco* magazine. She has authored many HarperCollins Access Travel Guides, including the bestselling *California Wine Country*. Peck is the founder and editor of the travel site Celebration Traveler: At Home in the World (www.celebrationtraveler.com). Her work speaks to travelers setting out to connect on a deeper level with themselves, their loved ones and their environment.

Alec Scott is a Canadian expat based in Oakland. His work ranges widely from culture to travel, from business to technology to the law. A former lawyer, he has worked as an editor and columnist at *Toronto Life* magazine and as a producer at the Canadian Broadcasting Corporation. He has taught travel writing at Stanford. His outlets include *Sunset,* the *Los Angeles Times,* the *San Francisco Chronicle, The Guardian* and *Smithsonian* magazine. His long-form work has been nominated for 13 National Magazine Awards in Canada, winning three, and his travel pieces have won a North American Travel Journalists' Association gold and the Eureka! award.

Anne Sigmon's piece in this anthology, *Sierra Point,* was singled out by the judges for honorable mention. For her, exotic travel was the stuff of dreams until, at age 38, she married Jack, took tea with erstwhile headhunters in Borneo and climbed Mount Kilimanjaro. Even after a stroke and with an autoimmune illness, she still travels to wild places around the world, making her way to Botswana, Syria, Iran and Uzbekistan. Sigmon's essays and award-winning travel stories have appeared in outlets including *Good Housekeeping,* GeoEx.com, Best Travel Writing.com and in anthologies including *To Oldly Go: Souvenirs from the Inner Journey* and *"Wandering in Cuba: Revolution and Beyond.*

Tom Wilmer is the author of three books and has produced travel features for NPR affiliate KCBX since 1989. His NPR.org podcast shows have won five SATW Lowell Thomas awards and more than 10 regional awards. In addition to video production and photography, Wilmer is Culture Editor at *360 Magazine* in L.A. and Travel Editor for NYC-based *Civilian Magazine.* Previous credits include Travel Editor, *Las Vegas Magazine;* Travel Editor, *Central Coast Magazine;* and columnist, *Santa Rosa Press Democrat, Tahoe Quarterly* and *Arizona Foothills.* He was the winner of the prestigious Tourism Australia/Qantas Henry Lawson Travel Writing Award for a nine-page Aussie Outback feature in *Cowboys & Indians* magazine.

The organization was started in 1984 in San Francisco, when a handful of aspiring travel writers met in one another's homes to share stories and critique each other's work. Less than a decade later, there were 30 members and a set of bylaws, and it has continued to grow.

Today, BATW is a professional organization of 120 travel writers and photographers, sharing our experiences in words and pictures in every medium, from print to podcasts, from blogs to YouTube video channels. We are a 501(c) nonprofit offering monthly educational programs in some of the most exciting venues in Northern California, or (these days) by Zoom.

To learn more and attend a meeting, go to www.batw.org or send an email to president@batw.org.

CPSIA information can be obtained
at www.ICGtesting.com
Printed in the USA
FSHW020416251020
75105FS